HERS ANCIENT AND MODERN

WOMEN'S WRITING IN SPAIN AND BRAZIL

HERS ANCIENT AND MODERN

WOMEN'S WRITING IN SPAIN AND BRAZIL

edited by
CATHERINE DAVIES and JANE WHETNALL

Hers Ancient and Modern: Women's Writing in Spain and Brazil, edited by
Catherine Davies and Jane Whetnall

The rights of the contributors in this work have been asserted by them in
accordance with the Copyright, Designs and Patents Act, 1988.

First published by Manchester Spanish & Portuguese Studies, 1997.

Reprinted in facsimile by SPLASH Editions, 2019.

The editors wish to acknowledge the generosity of the following bodies who
helped to fund the conference on which this volume was based, and also the
original publication: The British Academy; The Spanish Embassy, London; The
Calouste Gulbenkian Foundation; The Institute of Romance Studies, University
of London; and the School of Modern Languages, Queen Mary and Westfield
College. They also wish to thank the Centro Cañada Blanch de Estudios
Hispánicos Avanzados, Manchester, where the volume was typeset.

Cover design by Hannibal.

ISBN 9781912399086

CONTENTS

In memory of Biruté Ciplijauskaité and Janet Pérez

PREFACE

TOO OFTEN, medieval, Golden-Age, and contemporary literary studies are deemed to be mutually exclusive. This volume demonstrates the usefulness – even the necessity – of a more flexible approach. It brings together a selection of essays originally read as papers at a two-day conference on women writers in Spain, Portugal, and Latin America from the Middle Ages to the present, organized in June 1995 by the editors and by Dr Abigail Lee Six at the Institute of Romance Studies, University of London. The scope of the conference was left deliberately wide in the hope that texts written by women would share sufficient points of contact for them to obviate or at least attenuate chronological and geographical divisions. In the event, that hope was realized in the range of papers offered and the exchange of ideas that resulted.

The authors represented here are widely removed from each other in time and space, covering medieval, Golden-Age, and contemporary Spain, as well as contemporary Brazil. Yet, as will become clear, the women studied contended in their writings with similar problems and in similar ways. Their juxtaposition in a single volume allows the reader to focus on the remarkable affinities in theme and strategy shared by women writers from diverse Hispanic and Lusophone contexts. Such features are the marks of identity of a long-standing and continuous tradition of female authorship. Without wishing to preclude discussion of common writing practices, some of them possibly gender-defined, the following points of comparison seem to us to be among the more interesting: female creativity, or, in a violent reversal of the nurturing role, female aggression; intertextuality; and what we shall term transcendency: that is, the urge to violate norms imposed by society.

Several concerns are common to more than one of the writers studied here. Mothering, associated with nurturing, figures in the work of nuns such as Constanza de Castilla and Teresa of Avila, each writing as the head of a female community. Elena Carrera presents Teresa of Avila's *Camino de perfección* as a text which did not belong to its writer but to its readers, in the tradition of popular guides to prayer offered as spiritual nourishment. At a time when many such devotional texts had become forbidden fruit for women and unlettered men, Teresa strategically justified her new book by addressing it to her spiritual daughters for consumption within the convent. In her essay on two fifteenth-century nuns, Dayle Seidenspinner-Núñez describes how Constanza de Castilla's meditations on the Passion of Christ focus on the Compassio – the parallel sufferings endured by his mother – and dwell on the maternal role of Christ as symbolized by the pelican who feeds the faithful with his blood. In contrast, and at the opposite end of the time scale, motherhood is presented as an act of female violence in the fiction of contemporary Brazilian author Lygia Fagundes Telles, as Maria Manuel Lisboa argues with reference to two short stories, 'Verde lagarto amarelo' and 'Natal na barca'. Here, stereotypes of the caring mother disintegrate before an apocalyptic vision of maternity as power and political murder. Here, infanticide, real or imagined, psychological or metaphorical, is the favoured realization of maternity.

Like Fagundes Telles, many women writers nurture fantasies of transgressing and exorcise these visions of power through writing. The reiteration, transformation, and subversion of previous texts and readings, usually produced by men, supply them with the means and the provocation. The very act of breaking silence was perceived as transgression, as Dayle Seidenspinner-Núñez explains, and was a source of deep anxiety to the deaf nun Teresa de Cartagena. One of her strategies was to arrogate male authority to herself, by citing from and identifying with the Church Fathers who were her precursors. Later writers were to address the problem more obliquely. For Judith Drinkwater, the empowerment of women as the controlling force of narrative (and as readers outside the text) can be shown in one of María de Zayas's *Desengaños amorosos*, in which the heroine who exerts her power in pursuit of pleasure embodies and exemplifies the narrator's call for women to take up the sword as well as the pen in their own defence. Zayas's strategy in this case involves the rewriting of a classic myth and the literary tradition which exploited it, with a role reversal that reverberates outward from the central plot.

The concept of the canon, the body of sacred writings accepted as genuine and representative of the laws and principles set down by the Church, is as relevant today as it was in the medieval and early modern periods. For the Church we may substitute academic institutions, and the institutions responsible for the formation of the contemporary literary canon. Joan Brown and

Crista Johnson, in their survey of the Hispanic novel canon in the United States, reveal only too plainly the modest place allotted to women authors on recent graduate reading-lists. One of the factors that may have contributed to even the small measure of recognition accorded to three novels written by women is, they suggest, a susceptibility to multiple interpretation.

Two of the novelists who come top of their list are among those discussed in Janet Pérez's essay, which serves to illustrate the same point. As she demonstrates, a different kind of patriarchal discourse provides the intertexts for Spanish women writers during the era of Francoism and beyond. Teresa Barbero, Ana María Matute, Esther Tusquets, and Carmen Martín Gaite use fairy-tales and children's stories to expose the unreality of prescribed gender roles and to structure new rites of passage for their fictional characters. Phyllis Zatlin, meanwhile, questions the legitimacy and appropriateness of canonical critical labels in her exploration of the fantastic in the work of Cristina Fernández Cubas. With reference to two short-story collections, *El ángulo del horror* and *Ágatha en Estambul*, she shows how the author reworks the Gothic and the fantastic mode as defined by Todorov in order to incorporate realism, surrealism, and humour into her fiction. In Fernández Cubas's work, the figure of the mother may be rejected, as it is in the writings of Fagundes Telles. Of particular interest for this volume is Zatlin's account of 'El mundo', a story set in a post-war convent and featuring a narrator/protagonist who has no desire to leave but immerses herself in a world of story-telling (produced for internal consumption) and, ultimately, misreadings.

A different kind of intertextual strategy is employed by Hilary Owen who draws on Hélène Cixous's readings of James Joyce and Clarice Lispector in a comparative feminist analysis of Joyce's short story 'The Dead' and Lispector's 'A partida do trem'. Owen shows how Lispector goes further than Joyce in the expression of subjective disintegration: 'The Dead' concludes where 'A partida do trem' begins. The key to Lispector's radical approach is her particular use of interior monologue in an *écriture féminine* which reveals the instability of subjectivity while evoking multiple sensuality.

All the writers discussed in this volume strive, in one way or another, to transgress or transcend the boundaries of reality. These aspirations are, of course, not gender-specific, although the writing strategies they adopt in order to achieve them may well be. The modes of mysticism, of the fantastic, of Gothic horror, and of the fairy-tale suggest dissatisfaction with the limitations of the real, a gesturing towards another world, another way of thinking and being: what Mexican author Rosario Castellanos described in her famous poem 'Meditación en el umbral' as 'otro modo de ser humano y libre | otro modo de ser'. In a modern context, Biruté Ciplijauskaité shows how the poetry of María Victoria Atencia and María Sanz encapsulates this desire to transcend. Drawing on Gaston Bachelard's theories of creative imagination in relation to the masculine and the feminine, and Husserl's phenomenology of perception, she examines the ways in which María Sanz creates palimpsests to achieve transcendency through the contemplation of beauty – how she creates a woman's vision of 'landscapes with soul'. Sublimation of a different order informs the writings of contemplatives like Constanza de Castilla who embraces her femaleness as a sign of closeness to Christ, Teresa de Cartagena who rejoices in the deafness that cuts her off from the world, and Teresa of Avila who believed that her sustenance and inspiration came directly from the words of God.

Many more connections could be made between these essays; the pursuit of these is now in the hands of the interested reader. It remains to be said that this book would not have been possible without the help of many individuals and institutions. In particular we should like to thank two colleagues at the Department of Hispanic Studies, Queen Mary and Westfield College, University of London: Dr Abigail Lee Six, who spent many hours collaborating with us in the organization of the conference, and Dr Charles Davis. We should also like to thank all those who attended and participated in the conference and the home institutions which funded their visit. Special thanks are due to Mrs Simona Cain, formerly of the Institute of Romance Studies, who administered the conference impeccably.

CATHERINE DAVIES & JANE WHETNALL

Queen Mary College, London and
Institute of Modern Languages Research, University of London

'BUT I SUFFER NOT WOMAN TO TEACH':
TWO WOMEN WRITERS IN
LATE-MEDIEVAL SPAIN

DESPITE ST PAUL'S INJUNCTION (I Tim. 2:12) proscribing the speech of women, and despite the pervasive male gendering of medieval literary theory and practice, several women wrote religious texts in fifteenth-century Spain.[1] This paper will focus on the literary strategies of two writers, Teresa de Cartagena and Constanza de Castilla. Both Constanza and Teresa were from powerful and influential families, both were exceptionally well-educated women, both entered the convent as a result of external circumstances, both were contemporaries writing about 1460, and each places herself prominently in her own text.

* * * * *

'Yo, Constança': The Abbess as mother in the *Devoçionario* of Constanza de Castilla

CONSTANZA DE CASTILLA is a third-generation casualty of the civil war between Peter I of Castile and his bastard half-brother Henry of Trastamara, which ended in 1369 when Henry murdered Peter at Montiel. Recognizing that the greatest threat to their control of the throne came from within their own family, the Trastamaras sought to consolidate their succession by negotiating in 1388 the marriage of Henry III (grandson of the usurper Henry II) to Catherine of Lancaster (the granddaughter of Peter I and his first wife, Blanche of Bourbon). As part of the politically charged marriage agreement, Prince John (son of Peter I and his second wife, Juana de Castro) was to be

---

1. See Deyermond (1983), López Estrada (1986), Mirrer (1989), and Surtz (1995).

returned to Spain where he was immediately imprisoned for life in Soria. He married the daughter of his gaoler and fathered two children, Pedro and Constanza. Constanza probably entered the Convent of Santo Domingo el Real in Madrid in 1406 or 1408 and served as prioress from 1416 to 1465; she died in 1478 and was buried in the convent.[2]

Constanza's *Devoçionario* survives in a single manuscript (Madrid, Biblioteca Nacional, MS 7495). As it is not generally accessible, its contents are listed below:

Oraçión de la vida y passión de Iesús (fols 1r – 31r)
Prayers in Latin
    'O sapiencia que ex ore altissimi' (31v – 41v)
    Oración a la encarnación de Iesu Christo (41v – 44r)
De las oras de los clavos
    Latin version (44r – 58v)
    Version in *romançe* (58v – 75r)
Los quinze gozos de la gloriosa Virgen Santa María (75r – 78r)
Las siete angustias de Nuestra Señora la Virgen María (78v – 79v)
Letanía de Nuestra Señora (79v – 82v)
Apology (82v – 83r)
Epistolary texts in Latin and Castilian: St Ignatius of Antioch, the Virgin Mary, St John (93v – 97r)
Capítulo de las preguntas que deven fazer al omne desque está en punto de la muerte (97r – 99r)
Supplicatio in die mortis (101r – 102v).[3]

The collection apparently serves two purposes: the instruction of the nuns under Constanza's care – 'todas las dueñas deste monesterio', for whom she prays (fol. 30r) – and a personal confession compiled towards the end of her life with a growing awareness of her own mortality and impending death.

The manuscript begins with the *Oraçión de la vida y passión de Iesús*, which is subdivided into forty-four chapters of uneven length but with an identical structure evident in Chapter 1:

---

2.   On Constanza, see Huélamo San José (1992) and Surtz (1995: 21 – 40).

3.   References to the *Devoçionario* are to the Madrid manuscript. I have supplied accents and punctuation. My thanks to Constance Wilkins, who is currently preparing a critical edition of the *Devoçionario*, for generously providing me with a xerox of the manuscript.

Capítulo primero. Ihesu, miserere mei. Por virtud de la tu santa encarnación quando te plogo desçender del seno del padre en el sagrario de la
Virgen gloriosa tomando de sus entrañas vestidura de omne. Estoviste
allí nueve meses ençerado. Señor, pues por mí tu virtud plogo a ti, Verbo
de Dios, tanto humillarte a vestir tan pobre vestidura e suplico a ty por la
grandeza de la tu humildat que me libre del pecado de la sobervia en la
qual muchas vezes caygo por mi culpa. E dame virtud de humildat conplida por que yo conosca la grant miseria mía commo David: Quia ego
sum pulvis cinis vermis et non homo opprobrium hominum et abieccio
plebbis.

(fol. 1r)

Constanza opens each chapter with an apostrophe in Latin ('Ihesu, miserere
mei'; with the occasional variant, 'Ihesu, parce michi') and recounts an event
in Christ's life from the Incarnation to his final Ascension ('Por virtud de la tu
santa encarnación...'). She then interjects herself into the text ('Señor, pues
por mí tu virtud plogo a ti...') and petitions for a virtue associated with a
biblical figure or saint ('E dame virtud de humildat conplida... commo
David'). By repeatedly placing herself in events from the life of Christ, Constanza serves as an accessible reference point for her convent sisters and facilitates and personalizes their participation in the narrative.

While the *Oración* recalls significant events of Christ's entire earthly existence, it focuses extensively on his Passion and Death, recounting in lingering
detail his suffering. The work rapidly passes through the Incarnation, Nativity,
Circumcision, Presentation, Flight into Egypt, Baptism, and Temptation in the
Wilderness (Chapters 1–8, fols 1r–4r), and then decelerates to evoke in
greater and more graphic detail incidents of Christ's Passion: the Arrest, the
Mocking, and the Crucifixion (see Surtz 1995: 62). A disproportionate
amount of text (Chapters 9–38, fols 4r–25r) covers the three-day period from
the Last Supper to Christ's Entombment, and the remaining six chapters (fols
25v–30r) recount the Harrowing of Hell, the Resurrection, the Ascension,
and Pentecost. Surtz has noted that, beginning with the chapters recounting
Christ's Death on the Cross, the narrative part of the text includes extensive
quotations in Latin from the corresponding Divine Offices. The interpolation
of liturgical material draws on the immediate reality of the nuns' own religious practices, for prayer and the singing of the Divine Offices were a crucial
part of the daily routine of the convent community. Like Constanza's appear

ance in the events of Christ's life, material from the liturgy would enhance the immediacy and accessibility of the account of Christ's suffering.

Constanza relates the theme of Christ's anguish more directly to her convent audience by emphasizing the Compassio, the parallel suffering endured by the Virgin as she witnesses the Crucifixion (Surtz 1995: 53). In the Incarnation narrative (Chapter 1), Constanza had conventionally attributed Christ's humanity to Mary ('tomando de sus entrañas vestidura de omne').[4] This accords with medieval physiological theories that, at conception, the female provides the physical matter of the foetus and the male the life or spirit, and with theological notions that just as Eve came from the matter of Adam so Christ came from the matter of Mary (Bynum 1982: 133).

In late medieval theology, Mary was the source and vessel of Christ's physicality: the flesh Christ put on was in some sense female because it was his mother's. Whichever theory of conception a theologian held, Christ, who had no earthly father, had to be seen as taking his flesh from Mary (Bynum 1987: 265). Constanza dramatically exploits this concept in Chapter 32 as the crucified Christ displays to his mother 'las llagas que tenías en la vestidura que della tomaste' (fol. 16v). A deeply affective description of the physicality of his Passion is proffered by Mary's posture at the foot of the Cross, where her open arms, slumped body, and downcast head mirror the body of Christ on the Cross: 'E la Dolorosa, tu madre, sus braços abiertos, su cuerpo encorvado, obedeçió tu mandamiento, su cabeça inclinada' (fol. 17r). This bond of suffering humanity between mother and son culminates in Mary's Compassio as her own heart is rent. She, also, is pierced with a blade and martyred:

> E acatando en ti con grandíssimo amor su coraçón fue rasgado, traspasado con cuchillo agudo, su ánima ensangustiada en tanto grado que la señora reçibió martirio de dolores, ca ella sintió los tormentos que tú reçebiste propiamente contigo, así commo una mesma carne.[5]

(fol. 17v)

The figurative crucifixion of Mary is again dramatized in the following text, *Las oras de los clavos*. Contemporary historical documents refer to a famous

---

4.   Compare Margaret of Oingt, who, like Hildegard of Bingen, wrote that Mary is the *tunica humanitatis*, the clothing of humanity that Christ puts on.

5.   Compare Catherine of Siena, who writes of Mary's sorrow at the Crucifixion: 'Oh sweetest love, which was the sword that pierced the heart and soul of the mother! The Son was broken in body, and the mother similarly, for his flesh was from her. Indeed, it is just that she suffered in what befell him for his flesh was from her' (Letter 30, cited in Bynum 1987: 265).

fiesta in Madrid to honour 'Los santos clavos', celebrated at the Convent of Santo Domingo as a papal concession to Constanza (Huélamo San José 1992). The second text in the *Devoçionario*, therefore, would be the *ofiçio* that Constanza composed to commemorate this fiesta. *Las oras de los clavos* celebrates the suffering humanity of Christ: his body broken and penetrated by the nails, and his blood spilled because of his love for humankind. The text emphasizes Christ's humble acceptance of his unjust torment, the love of the Father who offers his Son for our salvation, and the Compassio of the Virgin.

Constanza praises the nails that pierce Christ's flesh because the pain they inflicted effected humankind's redemption. She graphically recreates Christ's agony through Mary's Compassio:

> Miravas tú, señora, continamente con grandíssimo dolor & con angustia indicibile al tu dulce fijo en la Cruz elevado, todo descoïuntado de tres clavos colgado, de sí deramante toda la sangre del su cuerpo precioso en precio de nuestra redempçión. E quando tú sentías las gotas de sangre sobre tu cabeça coriente non siento yo coraçón que pueda pensar nin lengua que pueda contar quanto con el dolor que tú, piadosa madre, padecías. El tu coraçón en esse tienpo fue todo llagado, ansí commo las manos & los pies del tu fijo. Creemos verdaderamente sin dubda que aquellos tres clavos que en la cruz al tu fijo traspasaron a ti no perdonaron, mas propiamente dentro en tu coraçón fueron fincados con aquellos mesmos dolores, los quales el fijo tuyo en la tu propia carne padescía, la qual de ti verdaderamente avía tomado. E ansí traspasaron & quebrantada con muy grandes & indicibiles dolores en grado soberano ... martirio reçebiste.
>
> (fols 65v – 66r)

The *Oraçión* insists on the graphic physicality of Christ's death. The fruitfulness of his suffering is evoked through the figure of the pelican:

> Ihesu, miserere mei. Por la llaga que fue fecha en tu costado quando tú, verdadero pelicano, consentiste a Longinos que la abriese con la lança e manó sangre e agua ...
>
> (fol. 22r)

The image of Christ as 'verdadero pelicano' is repeated twice in *Las oras de los clavos*: 'El verdadero pelicano fue muerto en la cruz por vivificar con la sangre suia los fijos que eran muertos' (fol. 68v; see also fol. 72v). In the bestiary tradition, the pelican was reputed to rip open its breast to feed its young. In medieval physiology, the image is often applied to the loving mother who, like the pelican, nurtures her child with her own blood (in medieval medical theory, breast milk was considered to be processed blood). In religious iconography, Christ the 'verdadero pelicano' sacrifices his blood to nurture his children:

> Both men and women writers saw Christ's body on the Cross, which in dying fed the world, as in some sense female. Again, physiological theory reinforced image. To medieval natural philosophers, breast milk was transmuted blood, and a human mother – like the pelican that also symbolized Christ – fed her children from the fluid of life that coursed through her veins. As early as the second century, Clement of Alexandria had spoken of Christ as mother, drawing the analogy between a God who feeds humankind with his own blood in the Eucharist and a human mother whose blood becomes food for her child.
>
> (Bynum 1987: 270)

The maternal imagery is particularly apposite to Constanza's presentation of God, stressing his creative power, and his love and presence in the physical body of Christ and in the flesh and blood of the Eucharist.[6]

Late-medieval theological interpretations of the Eucharist provide an important subtext for the *Oración*, which Constanza states was intended to be recited prior to Communion ('Dévese dezir esta oraçión ante de la comunión', fol. 1r). Notions of the Eucharist shifted fundamentally from the time of the early Church to the later Middle Ages.[7] Although theologians and visionaries never forgot that the bread on the altar was the memorial of a communal Passover meal and of Old-Testament sacrifice, they increasingly emphasized the Eucharist as suffering and bleeding flesh. As the thirteenth and fourteenth centuries wore on, theologians came to place the saving moment of Christian history in the Crucifixion rather than in the Incarnation or Resurrection. Late medieval theology taught that, at the central moment of Christian ritual, the moment of consecration, God became food that is body. In becoming flesh, God takes on humanity, and that humanity saves, not by being,

---

6. 'The association of Christ's flesh with woman was reinforced in iconography, where Mary had a place of honour on eucharistic tabernacles. [There are] a number of late medieval instances in which a figure of Mary actually *is* the tabernacle in which the consecrated host is reserved ... In the so-called *Vierges ouvrantes*, statues of Mary opened to reveal the Trinity inside, thus underlining the notion that Mary is the container (i.e. the womb, the tabernacle, the reliquary) within which rests the body of God' (Bynum 1987: 268).

7. The following section on the Eucharist includes paraphrased statements from Bynum's chapter 'The Meaning of Food: Food as Physicality' (1987: 245-59).

but by being broken. It was only by bleeding, by being torn and rent, by dying, that Christ's body redeemed humanity. To eat Christ is to become Christ, and the Christ one becomes in the reception of Communion is the bleeding and suffering Christ of the Cross. The flesh of Jesus – both flesh as body and flesh as food – is at the centre of female piety in the late Middle Ages.

Certain devotional emphases, particularly devotion to Christ's suffering humanity and to the Eucharist, were characteristic of women's religious practices and writing in the late Middle Ages and are central themes in Constanza's *Devoçionario*. Her collection of prayers, liturgical offices, tracts, hymns, and letters comprises a miscellany assembled for the use and instruction of her convent sisters. Doctrine is made more accessible through a network of maternal metaphors, through Constanza's affective spirituality centering on the humanity of Christ and the maternity of the Virgin, and through the feminization of religious language – all evidence of what Arenal and Schlau (1989a, 1989b) see as the woman-centredness of convent writing.

Constanza's writing is further characterized by the easy and frequent placing of herself in her texts: on several occasions she herself assumes the mediatory role of Mary and intercedes on behalf of the souls of her deceased relatives (fol. 26r), on behalf of the beleaguered Henry IV (fol. 27v), and on behalf of the nuns under her charge and guidance (fols 29v – 30r). Her frequent and direct self-naming – 'Yo Constança' – establishes her position and authority as a member of a royal line, as the prioress/protector/teacher of her convent, as an exemplary sinner (fol. 31v), and as the author of her texts which she claims as her own and submits to the authority of the Church (fols 82v – 83r). This female voice could be readily taken over by other nuns of her convent as well as by a more general female readership (Surtz 1995: 49).

The *Devoçionario* opens with Constanza's extended prayer on the life – and particularly the Passion and Death – of Christ. To the extent that it was Christ's humanity, derived from Mary, that suffered the Passion, women could identify with his suffering. As we have seen, Constanza explores the Passion in greater detail than other events of Christ's life. Thus, Christ's preparation for his death serves as a model to help the individual sinner, and specifically Constanza, to prepare for her own death (Surtz 1995: 63).

Moreover, the humanity redeemed by Christ was associated with woman rather than man. Woman symbolized the physical, lustful, material, appetite-driven part of human nature, and man symbolized spiritual, rational, or mental human faculties. In so far as Christ became human to save sinners, women writers could draw from the traditional notion of the female as physical humanity an emphasis on their own redemption. Both sinful and saved humanity were imagined as feminine:

> For it was human beings as *human* (not as a symbol of the divine) whom Christ saved in the Incarnation; it was body as flesh (not as spirit) that God became most graphically on the altar; it was human suffering (not human power) that Christ took on to redeem the world.
>
> (Bynum 1987: 296)

Thus, Constanza concludes with the highly personal *Supplicatio in die mortis*: 'porque el término de mi vida se acaba, necesario es dar cuenta' (fol. 101r). She characteristically places herself directly into her text ('Yo Constanza me confieso a ti...'), recalls the imagery of Christ's agony and sacrifice from the opening *Oraçión*, and offers her final petition for mercy:

> Señor, miénbrate que el preçio de mi ánima es la sagrada sangre tuia que por cinco partes de tu cuerpo salió abondosa con espantosos & graves dolores fasta que te fizieron dar el spíritu... Suplico con aquella omilldat & reverençia que puedo de la sentencia que meresçen mis culpas para ti mesmo, Ihesu, redemptor mío et iuez mío, mediator deus & homo qui me acates & me iuzgues segund la grandeza de la tu grand misericoria.
>
> (fol. 102v)

*   *   *   *   *

'Mi grosero juyzio mugeril' : Teresa de Cartagena, *Arboleda de los enfermos*

TERESA DE CARTAGENA belonged to the most influential and powerful *converso* family in late-medieval Spain. Throughout the fifteenth and sixteenth centuries, the Cartagena/Santa María clan was pivotal in the political, religious, economic, and literary culture of Castile. Teresa was probably born between 1415 and 1420 and grew up in the family home in Burgos. The little we know about her may be culled from scattered details in her manuscript: she was afflicted with deafness, probably in her late teens, she entered a convent, was in constant poor health, and spent much of her time alone, reading and meditating. She wrote two works: *Arboleda de los enfermos*, a treatise on the spiritual benefits of affliction and patience, and *Admiraçión operum Dey*, a defence of her writing.[8]

Unlike Constanza, there is no reference in Teresa's works to her convent sisters nor to convent life. To combat her loneliness, in *Arboleda*, she addresses, instead, an allegorical community of fellow sufferers, the Convent of the Afflicted. Unlike Constanza, Teresa – marginalized by her sex, her deafness, and perhaps her status as a *conversa* – exemplifies the 'anxiety of authorship' Sandra Gilbert and Susan Gubar have analysed in *The Madwoman in the Attic*:

> Thus the loneliness of the female artist, her feelings of alienation from male predecessors coupled with her need for sisterly precursors and successors, her urgent sense of her need for a female audience together with her fear of the antagonism of male readers, her culturally conditioned timidity about self-dramatization, her dread of the patriarchal authority of art, her anxiety about the impropriety of female invention – all these phenomena of 'inferiorization' mark the woman writer's struggle for creation from those of her male counterparts.
>
> (Gilbert & Gubar 1979: 50)

Applying this paradigm to Teresa, the loneliness of being a female artist would only be exacerbated by her deafness. As for the attendant alienation from male predecessors and need for sisterly precursors and successors, Teresa's deafness cut her off from the oral female sub-culture (women's songs, proverbs, convent chatter – the convent culture of Constanza) and thrust her into the dominant culture of male letters. Her urgent need for a female audience (Teresa directs both her texts to an unnamed reader: 'virtuosa señora', presumably Doña Juana de Mendoza), together with her fear of the antagonism of male readers (implicit in certain literary strategies in *Arboleda* and subsequently realized in its hostile reception), her culturally conditioned timidity about self-dramatization (Teresa obliquely dramatizes herself through her literary authorities), her dread of the patriarchal authority of art (the 'prudentes varones' as she refers to her detractors in *Admiraçión*), her anxiety about the impropriety of female invention (the formulaic repetition of disclaimers like 'the lowliness and grossness of my womanly mind', 'my

---

8.   On Teresa, see Deyermond (1976–77 and 1983), Ellis (1981), López Estrada (1986), Marimón Llorca (1990), Molina (1990), Rodríguez Rivas (1992), Seidenspinner-Núñez (1994), Surtz (1987 and 1995: 1–20), Vicente García (1989). References to *Arboleda* are to Hutton's edition (Teresa de Cartagena 1987: 37–109). I have identified Biblical quotations in the text.

poor womanly intellect', 'my coarse womanly judgement'): all these phenomena of inferiorization mark Teresa's struggle for artistic self-definition in *Arboleda de los enfermos*.

As anxiety-ridden as her nineteenth-century sisters examined by Gilbert and Gubar, Teresa applies several strategies obliquely to lend authority to her own text. She addresses *Arboleda de los enfermos* to the 'virtuous lady' who has presumably requested its composition, a strategy that serves two rhetorical functions: it takes responsibility from Teresa since she is acceding to a request to write rather than initiating the act of writing of her own accord, and the inclusion of the figure of an accessible and receptive female reader facilitates communication to a more general audience.

Another strategy is the use of gendered humility formulas by way of a *captatio benevolentiae*:

> E como la baxeza e grosería de mi mugeril yngenio a sobir más alto non me consienta, atreviéndome a nobleza e santidat del muy virtuoso Rey e Profeta llamado Davit, comyenço a buscar en su devotísymo cançionero, que *Salterio* se llama, algunas buenas consolaçiones.
>
> Mas porque mi grosero juyzio mugeril haze mis dichos de pequeña o ninguna abtoridat...

(Teresa de Cartagena 1967: 38, 96)[9]

Teresa acknowledges her own inherent lack of authority as a woman by means of these inferiorizing self-references and then appropriates the voice of a male authority (David, Peter Lombard, Job) to lend authority to her own words.[10]

Arboleda de los enfermos has been read both as a work of self-consolation and as an attempt through the act of writing to overcome the isolation imposed by Teresa's deafness. While critics invariably emphasize the autobiographical dimension of Teresa's devotional treatise as distinctive to her work, *Arboleda de los enfermos* has not been critically examined as a piece of

---

9. The second passage leads to quotations from Peter Lombard and from Job.

10. A comparison between *Arboleda* and Teresa's principal source, Pedro de Luna's *Libro de las consolaciones de la vida humana* (see Gayangos's 1884 edition), illustrates how she appropriates male discourses of authority. Luna addresses his book outwardly to 'tú', a younger male reader he purports to instruct; a conventional hierarchy of authority is established whereby the moralist narrator directs the reader he has identified in the text. Teresa's first-person narrator assumes the more intimate voice of a confessional work directed inwardly, exploring her own personal experience as an example. The hierarchy of authority that structures Luna's *Libro* is missing in Teresa's text as she strives to establish a community with her fellow infirm: the 'Convento de las Dolençias'.

women's writing. I am not suggesting that Teresa set out consciously to write a conventional autobiography proceeding from childhood to conversion to religious maturity; instead, she intricately weaves together her life and her texts and represents herself obliquely rather than explicitly.

There are several specific examples of Teresa's oblique autobiography in *Arboleda*. The first is the initial inclusion of herself in her text:

> Grand tienpo ha, virtuosa señora, que la niebla de tristeza tenporal e humana cubrió los términos de mi bevir e con un espeso torvellino de angustiosas pasiones me llevó a vna ýnsula que se llama 'Oprobrium hominum et abiecio plebis' [Ps. 21: 7] donde tantos años ha que en ella bivo, si vida llamar se puede... Asý que en este exillyo e tenebroso destierro, más sepultada que morada me sintiendo, plogo a la misericordia del muy Altýsimo alunbrarme con la luçerna de su piadosa graçia... E con esta Luz verdadera que alunbra a todo omne que viene [e]n este mundo [John 1: 9], alunbrado mi entendimiento, desbaratada la niebla de mi pesada tristeza, vi esta ýnsula ya dicha ser buena e saludable morada para mí.

$$(37-38)$$

Here Teresa represents her past history of illness and suffering in terms of an allegorical landscape: she is metaphorically swept away to an island called 'The Scorn of Mankind and Outcast of the People'. By means of an allegorical construct Teresa can elaborate figuratively the initial loneliness, despair, and suffering she had experienced when she became deaf, without focusing on her specific personal circumstances.

A different obliqueness in Teresa's self-representation occurs in her exhortation to her fellow sufferers to endure virtuously their afflictions:

> Todo el bien deste mundo es manjar de los sanos; pues dexemos lo ajeno y usemos de nuestra dieta, y de tales viandas gustemos que nos hagan buen estómago, sofridor de todo trabajo. De seys viandas me paresçe que devemos y podemos usar seguramente todos los que dolençias padesçemos. Las quales son éstas: tribulada tristeza, paçiençia durable, contriçión amarga, confesión verdadera y frequentada, oraçión devota, perseveraçión en obras virtuosas.

$$(62)$$

Here Teresa notes that worldly pleasures are reserved for the healthy; the infirm are seated at a different table and presented with a different menu. She encourages her fellow sufferers to eat of their own bitter fare, for what is physically disagreeable is spiritually beneficial. Then, seemingly disheartened, she complains of the fare she has been served in life: 'E yo no sé para qué queremos los enfermos cosa deste mundo ca bien que rodeemos, no halleremos en él cosa que bien nos quiera' (Teresa de Cartagena 1967: 63). Embedded in Teresa's allegorical Supper of the Infirm is a deeply personal – and obliquely autobiographical – revelation of painful family rejection:

> Los plazeres que en él son del todo nos haboreçen, la salut nos desanpara, los amigos nos olvidan, los parientes se enojan, e aun la propia madre se enoja con la hija enferma, y el padre aboresçe al hijo que con continuas dolençias le ocupare la posada.
>
> (63)

In *Arboleda*, Teresa writes about herself through her texts rather than through specific references. Here we must remember that so much of what we know about Teresa actually comes from the initial rubrics to her texts:

> Este tractado se llama *Arboleda de los enfermos*, el qual conpuso Teresa de Cartajena seyendo apasyonada de graves dolençias, espeçialmente aviendo el sentido del oýr perdido del todo.
>
> (37)

> Aquí comiença un breve tractado el qual co[n]vinientemente se puede llamar *Admiraçión operum Dey*. Conpúsole Teresa de Cartajena, religiosa de la horden de [   ] a petiçión e ruego de la Señora Doña Juana de Mendoça, muger del Señor Gomes Manrique.
>
> (111)

Ironically, when we first read *Arboleda*, we have an excess of circumstantial information – probably provided by the copyist – that Teresa did not intend her readers to have. In contrast, Teresa's own text is marked by an erasure of the circumstantial: unlike Constanza, she never names herself, never explicitly reveals her profession as a nun, never divulges details of her family, never provides any personal details, and any self-references are presented either obliquely or figuratively. This anonymity permits Teresa greater freedom to elaborate the autobiography of her spiritual life and also magnifies her exemplarity, for the suppression of concrete personal details circumvents her limited symbolic value as an afflicted woman and casts her instead as a more universal exemplar of suffering humanity. Thus, she constructs herself largely through literary analogues, generally male biblical figures and male biblical voices (David, Job, the blind man on the road to Jericho, Lazarus, and ultimately Christ): the self of a faithful sinner so beloved and chosen by God that He inflicts suffering to draw her closer to Him, to protect her from the dangers of this world, and thus to prepare her for salvation. This is a culturally valued fiction of male selfhood, a biblical myth rehearsed over and over again in the stories of the Old Testament and particularly in the Book of Job. Teresa's innovation is that the subject is female, and one of her strategies is to minimize the gendering of her own story by emphasizing its figurative spiritual dimension –where male and female are theoretically equivalent– over its literal details (see McLaughlin 1974).

Medieval gender ideologies established correspondences between female sexuality, female speech, and female goodness predicated on the ideals of silence (closed mouth), virginity or chastity (closed womb), and enclosure in house or convent (see Stallybrass 1986: 126–27). In her writing, Teresa figuratively associates her deafness with her entering the convent: God closed her ears to human voices, cloistering her hearing ('las claustras de mis orejas') and enclosing her in a community of suffering ('el convento de las dolençias'). Although Teresa's figurative convent of suffering has more thematic presence in her work than her physical convent, medieval notions of the woman religious inform her self-representation and her writing deeply.

The imposition of Teresa's deafness initiates a process of cloistering (enclosure and reclusion) that rhetorically establishes her 'goodness' by distancing her from misogynous paradigms of woman and symbolically enables her assumption of masculinity, of human exemplarity. If, however, the closing of her ears is presented as an act of God, the subsequent closing of her mouth is presented as an act of Teresa. Her refusal to speak cloisters her from the outside world (she refuses worldly conversations and visits, 41–42) and cloisters her desire: she rechannels her desire from the worldly to the spiritual (42) and reconciles her desire with her suffering ('E yo, que fasta aquí quería e non podía enplear mi tienpo en las conversaçiones seglares e agora ya nin puedo nin quiero nin querría thener poder para conplir tan dañoso querer', 43). Teresa's own repression of speech completes the process initiated by her deafness by attaining full silence (ears and voice), full erasure from public life (no visits or conversations), full closure of the body (closed womb, closed ears, closed mouth), and full occlusion of worldly desire. Her exemplarity is compromised only in the transgressive act of breaking her silence and writing her story. Her awareness of this transgression is the source of her anxiety

concerning authorship and the literary strategies applied to negotiate that
anxiety (self-deprecating humility formulas, appropriation of male authorities,
involvement of a female reader, oblique autobiography, figurative positioning
of her self, double-voiced narrative structure). That her anxiety was well
founded is evident from the prologue to *Admiración operum Dey* where she
recounts the hostile reception of *Arboleda* by those 'prudentes varones' who
rejected a woman's access to writing and, more importantly, disputed Teresa's
authorship of her own autobiographical and devotional text.

This is the final difference between Teresa and Constanza: the pronoun-
ced absence of the woman-centredness characteristic of the *Devoçionario*,
clearly attributable to the isolation imposed by Teresa's deafness.[11] Bynum
notes (1987: 263) that women writers did not necessarily draw from the traditional notion of a symbolic dichotomy between male/spirit and female/flesh
any sense of incapacity for virtue, for spiritual growth, or for salvation. In
their religious texts, women writers tended either to neutralize their own gender – the literary strategy of Teresa de Cartagena – or, like Constanza de
Castilla, embrace their femaleness as a sign of closeness to Christ.

DAYLE SEIDENSPINNER-NÚÑEZ

University of California, Irvine

---

11. What is extraordinary in Teresa's devotional text is the absolute lack of mention of
female exemplars, particularly of the Virgin Mary, the loving maternal mediator markedly
absent even in *Admiraçión*, where Teresa defends the possibility of women receiving acts of
divine grace (the Virgin being a conventional presence in pro-feminist defences in the late
Middle Ages). This is all the more remarkable when we consider Teresa's family name
(Cartagena/Santa María) and the tradition of her family coat of arms which recorded the clan's
purported descent from the Virgin. Although the Virgin is prominently cited in Teresa's source
text, Pedro de Luna's consolatory treatise, her presence in *Arboleda* is restricted to the headline
preceding the title – possibly added by the copyist – quite outside the boundaries of Teresa's
text in which affective religiosity is vested, instead, in the patriarchal Father and in Christ.

INTERTEXTUALITY IN TERESA OF AVILA'S
CAMINO DE PERFECCIÓN

CAMINO DE PERFECCIÓN stands out amongst Teresa of Avila's writings for the ironical and, on occasions, overtly polemical tone of many of its passages.[1] This text is in remarkable contrast with her first (and immediately preceding) book, *El libro de la vida*, which was full of apologetic claims and dominated by the rhetorical topos of the reluctant writer. The conspicuously unapologetic tone of the first version of *Camino* may seem surprising if one does not bear in mind the circumstances in which the text was written, at a time when any vernacular writing on spiritual matters, and especially on mental prayer, was regarded as suspect. Against a background of criticism of mental prayer, Teresa's text is produced precisely to defend that practice, from within the protective walls of the Convent of San José. It appears to have been written as a dialogue with a small community of nuns with whom Teresa could, as it were, gossip freely.

In *Camino* Teresa is writing from a clearly different standpoint from that of *Vida*, which was intended as a confession in which her confessors could examine her soul and experiences of prayer, to determine whether or not they were from God, before she could be permitted to make her first foundation of a Carmelite house according to the primitive Rule. Now, after three years of living in this foundation, the Convent of San José, of which she has become the prioress, Teresa has attained a position of power and authority. Since she has been a nun for longer than any of the others, she feels she can give them practical advice about prayer and convent life. Hence her emphasis on the nuns' expectations:

---

1.   The text exists in two versions, both of which, judging from internal evidence, seem to have been written in 1566, the year after *El libro de la vida* was completed. I shall refer to the earlier version as CE (Escorial Codex) and to the second as CV (Valladolid Codex) and, unless otherwise stated, quotations are taken from Efrén de la Madre de Dios and Otger Steggink's edition of the *Obras completas* (Teresa de Jesús 1986: 233–419), which sets out both texts, one above the other.

Sé que no falta el amor y deseo en mí para ayudar en lo que yo pudiere
para que las almas de mis hermanas vayan muy adelante en el servicio del
Señor; y este amor, junto con los años y espiriencia que tengo de algunos
monesterios, podrá ser aproveche para atinar en cosas menudas más que
los letrados que, por tener otras ocupaciones más importantes y ser
varones fuertes, no hacen tanto caso de cosas que en sí no parecen nada y
a cosa tan flaca como somos las mujeres todo nos puede dañar.

                              (CE Prologue 3; Teresa de Jesús 1986: 237)

This claim needs to be placed in its social context, in a century in which
women and laymen had been explicitly denied the right to teach doctrine and
many had been accused of Alumbradismo. Teresa feels obliged to justify her
own bold act of writing by stating that she will not interfere with the teaching
of learned theologians, but will rather be concerned with insignificant, trivial
matters for which they have no time and of which they have no experience,
since they are allegedly of a stronger nature and unconcerned with such
things. She is, in fact, well aware that, since she lacks the authority and the
learning of the *letrados* (theologians), she may be criticized for daring to write
on spiritual matters. There is evidence of such awareness in a passage crossed
out in the first version and omitted in the second, in which she alludes to the
suspicion with which the learned men of the Church looked upon the women
who led a spiritual life and dared to speak about it publicly:

¿No vasta, Señor, que nos tiene el mundo acorraladas... que no hagamos
cosa que valga nada por Vos en público ni osemos hablar algunas ver-
dades que lloramos en secreto...? No lo creo yo, Señor, de vuestra bon-
dad y justicia, que sois juez, y no como los jueces del mundo, que, como
son hijos de Adán y en fin todos varones, no hay virtud de mujer que no
tengan por sospechosa. Sí que algún día ha de haver, Rey mío, que se
conozcan todos. No hablo por mí, que ya tiene conocido el mundo mi
ruindad, y yo holgado que sea pública, sino porque veo los tiempos de
manera, que no es razón desechar ánimos virtuosos y fuertes, aunque
sean de mujeres.

                              (fols 11v–12r; 1965: II. 68)[2]

Camino thus appears to be a set of teachings for the nuns of San José about
convent life and the practice of appropriate virtue. But this occupies only the

---

2.   I am quoting here from Tomás Álvarez's facsimile edition – Teresa de Jesús (1965) –
since the Biblioteca de Autores Cristianos editors, claiming that this passage is illegible (1986:
249), do not include it in their text of CE.

first third of the book (Chapters 4–24). It then becomes a guide to mental prayer (Chapters 30–72) and a fervent defence of its practice, against the views of the Dominican Melchor Cano and other eminent scholastic theologians of her time. The core of the text is dedicated to the method of prayer known as *recogimiento* (Chapters 16–31) which Teresa has learned from Franciscan writings such as Francisco de Osuna's *Tercer abecedario espiritual* of 1527 and Bernardino de Laredo's *Subida del monte Sión* of 1535 or 1538, and which she has practised for over twenty years. The pretext she uses for writing on mental prayer is that the nuns wish her to: 'Diréis, mis hijas, que para qué os hablo en virtudes; que hartos libros tenéis que os las enseñan; que no queréis sino contemplación' (CE 24.3; 1986: 297). She feels confident to speak on the subject: 'Digo yo que, aun si pidiérais meditación, pudiera hablar de ella y aconsejar a todos la tuvieran' (CE 24.3; 1986: 297). But it is precisely this kind of confident claim which her censors chose to delete. This passage was suppressed from the second version of *Camino*, which was more carefully written with a view to reaching a broader readership and, unlike the first version, was authorized for circulation amongst Teresa's convents.

I also see *El libro de la Vida* both as a pretext and as an intertext in relation to Teresa's having dared to write *Camino* on the subject of mental prayer. Since her confessor, Domingo Báñez, had banned *Vida* from circulation, Teresa can offer *Camino* as a consolation for the nuns. She also uses her present text to advertise the absent one, rather than to replace it. Thus she makes claims such as the following – 'aunque por tenerlo escrito en otra parte, como he dicho, no me alargaré mucho en declararlo, diré algo' (CE 53.1; 1986: 363) – to make her reader the more eager to read that inaccessible book. She clearly judges that *Vida* is not only irreplaceable but also, and contrary to Báñez's opinion, essential reading for some of her nuns:

> Como está todo lo mijor dado a entender en el libro que digo tengo escrito (y ansí no hay que tratar de ello tan particularmente aquí; allí dije todo lo que supe); quien llegare a haverle Dios llegado a este estado de contemplación de vosotras –que, como dije, algunas estáis en él– procuradle, que os importa mucho de que yo me muera.

(CE 41.4; 1986: 339–40)

The words 'que os importa mucho de que yo me muera' are an allusion to the cautious attitude of Báñez, who took the view that, until her sanctity was proved after her death, no one could be sure that her experiences were inspired by God, and not by the devil.[3] Báñez's intention was to keep *Vida* out of circulation until he could be sure that her apparent sanctity would not prove fraudulent, as had happened with other women who had had trouble with the Inquisition during the previous five decades.[4] He was determined to wait and see whether or not Teresa would turn out to be a saint; as he put it, 'veremos en qué para esta mujer' (Santa Teresa 1935: I. 10). But Teresa does not seem to believe that *Vida* ought to be banned. She trusts that, if the new book is approved and considered to be appropriate reading for her nuns, Báñez will eventually allow them to read *Vida* too: 'el Padre fray Domingo Váñez... mi confesor... le tiene [*Vida*]. Si éste [*Camino*] está para que le veáis y os le da, también os dará el otro; si no, tomad mi voluntad, que con la obra he obedecido lo que mandastes' (CE 73. 6; 1986: 419).

The claim that she is acting in obedience to her nuns serves Teresa as a plea for having her writing authorized. Not being qualified to write, she has to delegate responsibility for doing so to her confessors, or, if this is not possible, then to her nuns. This is made very clear from the beginning:

> Sabiendo las hermanas de este monesterio de san Josef cómo tenía la licencia del padre presentado fray Domingo Vañes, de la Orden de santo Domingo, que al presente es mi confesor, para escrivir algunas cosas de oración, en que parece, por haver tratado muchas personas espirituales y santas, podré atinar, me han tanto importunado lo haga, por tenerme tanto amor, que aunque hay libros muchos que de esto tratan y quien sabe bien y ha sabido lo que escrive, parece la voluntad hace aceptas algunas cosas imperfectas y faltas más que otras muy perfectas; y como digo, ha sido tanto el deseo que las he visto y la importunación, que me he determinado a hacerlo, pareciéndome por sus oraciones y humildad querrá el Señor acierte algo a decir que les aproveche y me lo dará para que se lo dé.
>
> (CE Prologue 1; 1986: 236–37)

---

3.   Such proof might come from the presence of conventional signs such as a pervasive fragrance emanating from the tomb, incorruption of the flesh, and miracles.

4.   The first significant Inquisitorial investigations of spiritual women were of the Dominican Beata María de Santo Domingo in 1510. Teresa may not have been aware of the fates of women condemned by the Inquisition earlier in the century, but she certainly knew of the case of the Franciscan nun Magdalena de la Cruz, who in 1546 confessed to having simulated her mystical raptures and having been a victim of demonic delusion. Teresa herself was to face the Inquisition in 1575, after her book *Vida* had been reported to the Valladolid tribunal and she was charged with heretical practices before the Seville tribunal. The book obtained approval and she was left in peace after providing written reports on her method of prayer.

Teresa claims to have Báñez's permission to write, but there is no evidence that she ever obtained either his authorization or his approval. There are no traces of his handwriting in the margins of the manuscript, where other *letrados* made their suggestions. Even after Teresa's death, during the 1591 beatification proceedings, Báñez insisted that he had not read any of her books other than the first (*Vida*): 'de otros tratados y libros que andan impresos suyos no puede dar testimonio el dicho testigo, porque ni los ha leído impresos ni de mano' (Santa Teresa 1935: I. 10).

It is with the criticisms of her potential *letrado* readers, especially Báñez, in mind that she refers to the fact that she has discussed her practice of prayer with many persons known for their high spiritual achievement and their saintliness, and that they have given her the impression that she can write something appropriate on the subject ('podré atinar'). She sounds quite confident, despite her awareness, expressed later, that 'parece atrevimiento pensar yo he de ser alguna parte para alcanzar esto' (CE 4. 1; 1986: 249). She also tries to pre-empt possible objections to her writing on prayer on the grounds that there were already many books on prayer written by well-informed people – 'quien sabe bien y ha sabido lo que escrive' – by claiming that the nuns prefer texts which are not so polished, which contain 'algunas cosas imperfectas', and thus may be more accessible to them.

In contrast with learned authors who are used to planning the structure of their writing, Teresa declares that she does not know what she is going to write about. This, in the first place, will account for her disorderly style, but it will also be the necessary proof of the divine origin of the words she is inspired to write. On the one hand she claims that she writes fast, so she does not have the time to organize ('concertar') the inspired ideas into a coherent text, but, on the other, she does not think that she is qualified to write in the manner of a theologian. The whole enterprise of her writing about such matters seems unreasonable, 'desconcertada':

> Pienso poner algunos remedios para tentaciones de religiosas ... y lo que más el Señor me diere a entender, como fuere entendiendo y acordándoseme, que como no sé lo que será, no puedo decirlo con concierto; y creo que es mejor no le llevar, pues es cosa tan desconcertada hacer yo esto.

> (CE Prologue 2; 1986: 237)

Despite its being such an unreasonable idea, Teresa is determined to go ahead: 'pienso' is too much of an affirmation for the rest of her words to be taken as more than a rhetorical formula.

Teresa acknowledges the authority of some existing guides to prayer, but claims that they are only appropriate reading for those who are already spiritually advanced: 'para entendimientos concertados y almas que están ejercitadas y pueden estar consigo mesmas, hay tantos libros escritos y tan buenos y de personas tales, que sería yerro hiciésedes caso de mi dicho en cosas de oración' (CE 30. 1; 1986: 311). This is her way of arguing for the need for a work like hers, which, by addressing those readers with untrained minds ('entendimientos desbaratados'), may help fill the gap left by existing books:

> Mas de lo que yo querría tratar y dar algún remedio, si Dios quisiese acertase (y si no, al menos que entendáis hay muchas almas que pasan este travajo, para que no os fatiguéis las que al principio le tuvierdes, y daros algún consuelo en él), es de unas almas que hay y entendimientos tan desbaratados, que no parecen sino unos cavallos desbocados que no hay quien los haga parar: ya van aquí, ya van allí, siempre con desasosiego. Y aunque, si es diestro el que va en él, no peligra todas veces algunas sí; y cuando va seguro de la vida, no lo está del hacer cosa en él que no sea desdón; y va con gran travajo siempre.
>
> (CE 30. 2; 1986: 311 – 12)

Teresa's use of the expressions 'entendimientos desbaratados' and 'cavallos desbocados' to refer to her nuns is not without irony, since those were precisely the stereotypical images of women prevalent amongst the theologians of her time.

But Teresa can only allow herself this playfulness with views held outside the convent because she is writing to her nuns in confidence. The dialogue with them which she establishes in her text seems to be a continuation of everyday conversations in the convent: 'Muchas veces os lo digo, y ahora lo escrivo aquí; que en esta casa... huya mil leguas "razón tuve", "hiciéronme sinrazón", "no tuvo razón la hermana", ¡De malas razones nos libre Dios!' (CE 19. 1; 1986: 287). This writing in the manner of a dialogue is also shaped by her daily interactions with her nuns, whom she addresses mostly as 'hermanas', but sometimes also as 'amigas', or even 'hijas'.[5]

---

5.   The relationship of sisterhood is established from the beginning: '¡Oh hermanas mías en Cristo!...; no, hermanas mías, por negocios acá del mundo... No, hermanas mías, no es tiempo de tratar con Dios negocios de poca importancia' (CE 1. 5, CV 1. 5; see also CE 2. 1,

She makes it clear that she is not to be considered a source of 'authority', and that she cannot even perceive herself as such: 'ni sé cómo me pongo a hablar en ello. Es como quien oye hablar de lejos, que, aunque oye que hablan, no entiende lo que hablan' (CE 18.2; 1986: 260). Here she does not refer to any book in particular as the source of her knowledge, but stresses that she is speaking only of what she has learned from experience, or what God has taught her during prayer: 'no diré cosa que en mí u en otras no la tenga por espiriencia, u dada en oración a entender por el Señor' (CE Prologue 3; 1986: 237). In the second version, she even apologizes for her incoherence by claiming that God, at least, understands her difficult position as a writer: 'el Señor sabe la confusión con que escribo mucho de lo que escribo' (CV 25.4; 1986: 340).

Unlike Teresa's sixteenth-century readers (mostly nuns, priests, and pious members of the nobility), we do not need to resort to the argument of God's inspiration to explain the origins of her writing. Rather than look for origins, I propose to consider *Camino de perfección* as a text, or a 'tissue' – in the etymological sense stressed by Barthes 1977b: 160) – woven with references and echoes from a cultural context of which we can follow only some threads.

Teresa's sixteenth-century readers, in fact, could not regard her as an 'author', since that notion implied 'authority' and 'respect', both of which Teresa the writer lacked, at least in the eyes of the *letrados*. Her texts, nevertheless, circulated with her signature, her name, and this involved the necessary association of the worth of the texts with the figure of their writer, which was constructed (by her contemporaries and by herself) in terms of a set of values and prejudices concerning her femaleness, her lack of learning, and her yet-to-be-proved holiness. Rather than speaking, as does Foucault (1980), of the 'author-function', I would like to emphasize in this case the function of the writer's signature, especially since Teresa, in the tradition of biblical writers and of mystics, sees herself as the writer and God as the author of her text.

Many of the existing studies of Teresa of Avila's books place the focus on the originality of her writing as a saint or as a woman. These readings usually

---

6.4, 12.1). Occasionally the nuns are addressed as friends, as part of a pedagogical rhetoric: 'Creed, amigas, que sirviéndole vosotras como devéis' (CE 13.4). 'Hijas' is the form of address commonest in the second version of *Camino*, but already in the first Teresa addresses her nuns as a protective teaching mother: 'no se os olvide, hijas mías, por amor del Señor' (CE 2.1); 'hacernos pobres y no lo ser de espíritu...no plega a Dios, mis hijas' (CE 2.3); '¿Pensáis, hijas mías, que es menester poco para tratar con el mundo?' (CE 3.3); '¡Ay dolor de mí!... ¡qué mala tercera posistes, hijas mías...para que echase la petición por vosotras!' (CE 4.3).

presuppose a Romantic perception of the author as the origin, the nourisher of his book, and of the book as the author's child, the product of the author's individuality.[6] But this, in my view, is not the perception of author and text which prevailed in sixteenth-century spiritual writing. It is my contention that Teresa's contemporaries did not see the book as being nourished by its author, but, on the contrary, they perceived books as nourishment both for their readers and for their writers.

That the writer is primarily a reader is something of which Kristeva reminds us in her exposition of the Bakhtinian notion of writing, understood as a dialogue in which the writer is inevitably reading the other (Kristeva 1981: 68). For Bakhtin, the act of writing inserts history in the text, and the text in history. He sees the text as the result of an absorption and a reply to another text, belonging to an existing literary corpus (69). *Camino de perfección* can be seen as the network of words taken from various texts, oral as well as written, which cross the writer's subjectivity: a network which does not belong to her, but to her linguistic and socio-cultural context, and to the tradition of divinely inspired spiritual writing which she was following. Thus, rather than view Teresa of Avila's writing in post-Romantic terms as the output of an individual or a great saint, I prefer to see her texts as tissues woven from the words and ideas which had crossed her mind – or her soul, as she would put it – during prayer or during her reading. Her prayer is, in turn, a dialogue, a text woven with the intertexts of various spiritual writings which point towards God as the ultimate interlocutor. Teresa as a subject does not exist until ideas cross her mind; rather, her subjectivity is shaped by her constant dialogue with the ideas she receives.

However, the fact that Teresa of Avila believes that God is the ultimate interlocutor who gives her the words she writes does not mean that God is the actual source of her text, despite the conceptions of sixteenth-century writers who, like her, believed in divine authorship. Yet we may agree that Teresa was not an 'author' in the way we understand the term today. Using an image suggested by Barthes (1977a: 142), we may see Teresa's attitude to her writings as comparable to the attitude of the shaman who disclaims any responsibility for his narrative and gains admiration for his performance as an intermediary rather than for his originality. Her claims about the way she wrote

---

6.   This is precisely the kind of perception of author and text which Barthes tried to attack (1977a: 145).

also remind the modern reader of the automatic writing practised by surrealist poets, which Barthes treats as special cases. The analogy, however, cannot be pushed very far, since the surrealists were consciously subverting codes of writing, while Teresa, in my view, was not.

It may be more fruitful to look at how Teresa might have perceived her function as writer as that of providing nourishment. The idea of the text as nourishment was not an alien one for Teresa's contemporaries. It is an old image, used, for instance, in Petrarch's doctrine of imitation, which he illustrates by telling how he read the masters: 'Virgil, Horace, Livy, Cicero, not once but a thousand times... I ate in the morning what I would digest in the evening; I swallowed as a boy what I would ruminate upon as a man' (1966: 283). The digestive imagery which Petrarch uses to describe a writer's method of engaging with the work of his predecessors – imagery that can be traced back to Quintilian and Seneca – was very much present in sixteenth- and seventeenth-century discussions of imitation (Pigman 1980). Erasmus also uses it in his *Ciceronianus* to illustrate the notion of creative imitation:

> That which culls from all authors, and especially the most famous, what in each excels and accords with your own genius – not just adding to your speech all the beautiful things that you find, but digesting them and making them your own, so that they may seem to have been born from your mind and not borrowed from others, and may breathe forth the vigour and strength of your nature... so that your speech may not seem a patchwork, but a river flowing forth from the fount of your heart.
>
> (Erasmus 1910: 123)

The alimentary image was, in fact, a traditional one, already found in the Bible. There we find numerous passages praising the sweetness of the words of the Lord, such as the exclamation 'How sweet are thy words to my palate: more than honey to my mouth' (Ps. 119: 103). We also encounter the notion of literally eating the sacred text in passages from Ezekiel: 'And he said to me: Son of man, thy belly shall eat, and thy bowels shall be filled with this book, which I give thee. And I did eat it: and it was sweet as honey in my mouth' (Ezek. 3: 3) and from the Book of Revelation: 'And I took the book from the hand of the Angel, and ate it up: and it was in my mouth, sweet as honey' (Rev. 10: 10).

Threads of this biblical imagery also cross the texts of the Fathers of the Church. An example of this is St Augustine's suggestion in *De doctrina chris-*

tiana that the Holy Spirit 'with admirable wisdom and care for our welfare, so arranged the Holy Scriptures as by the plainer passages to satisfy our hunger, and by the more obscure to stimulate our appetite' (Augustine 1995: 37). And there are also texts which weave the patristic tissue further, as we can see, for instance, in Fray Francisco de Hevia's *Itinerario de la oración* of 1553:

> Y san Gregorio dice [*Sermones supra Ezequiel*, Book I, Sermo 10, n. 1]: hay algunos que cuando leen la sagrada escritura y penetran las altas sentencias de ella, que tienen en poco, menosprecian con desdén los mandamientos menores que son dados para los flacos y ignorantes. Por lo cual fue dicho al profeta: hijo del hombre, come todo lo que hallares. Como si le dijera más claramente: todo cuanto hay en la sagrada escritura es comestible espiritualmente, y por esto conviene que no deseches ninguna cosa, porque las cosas pequeñas componen la vida simple, y las cosas grandes levantan y avivezan la inteligencia. Lo de suso es de san Gregorio.
>
> (Hevia 1981: 140)

In the preface to this text there is a similar comparison between receiving knowledge and eating:

> En el libro de Ezequiel [Ezek. 3: 1] está escrito que hablando el Señor en espíritu con él, le dijo así: Hijo del hombre come este volumen y después que lo hubieres comido, ve y habla a los hijos de Israel. Por aquel volumen, el cual era a manera de envoltorio que estava escrito de dentro y de fuera, según dice el Nicolás de Lyra [*Expositiones morales*], puede ser entendido el conocimiento que daba Dios al profeta de las cosas que estaban por venir. El cual, abriendo la boca, dice el texto, que lo comió y le pareció por imaginaria visión que era más dulce que la miel, porque entendía lo que significaba y lo que le era revelado.
>
> (Hevia 1981: 139)

The theory of reading underlying this text is made the more interesting by the network of quotations which back it. Hevia takes a Franciscan interpretation of biblical *auctoritas* and uses it for his own purpose of demonstrating how, in an analogical way, one can acquire knowledge by eating, tasting, and savouring the words, the text of the paternoster, offered to us by the Lord:

> Pero declarando a mi propósito esta autoridad, has de saber, amantísimo lector en Jesu Cristo, que la sacratísima oración del paternóster, es así como un volumen o como un envoltorio que está escrito de dentro y de fuera por razón de las profundidades y muy grandes misterios que cada

palabra contiene. Y entonces se gusta y se come y se hace más dulce que miel cuando se entienden y se alcanzan a saber algunas cosas de ellas.

(Hevia 1981: 139)

The paternoster is, in fact, one of the threads Teresa uses to weave her teaching on mental prayer. She presents this vocal prayer as a safe haven for the nuns: 'haced bien, hijas, que no os quitarán el Paternóster y el Avemaría' (CE 36. 4; 1986: 326). These words were crossed out in the manuscript by the censor García de Toledo, who added his objection: 'parece que reprehende a los inquisidores que prohiben libros de oración'. There is, however, a further allusion to the paternoster being a safe prayer to meditate upon in the absence of devotional books which went uncensored: 'parece ha querido el Señor entendamos, hermanas, la gran consolación que aquí está encerrada y que cuando nos quitaren libros no nos pueden quitar este libro, que es dicho por boca de la mesma Verdad' (CE 73. 4; 1986: 418).

Teresa first suggests a meditation on the set words themselves, and then extends the tasting of those words into a more intimate and pleasurable experience of prayer, which she defends in the following terms: 'yo sé de unos y de otros, y sé claro que son intolerables los travajos que Dios da a los contemplativos; y son de tal arte que si no les diese aquel manjar de gusto no se podrían sufrir' (CE 28.2; 1986: 306). Bartolomeo di Domenico uses metaphors of the same kind to describe a similar method of meditation practised by Catherine of Siena: 'She was not concerned about reading a lot or saying many prayers. Rather she would chew on every single word, and when she found one she especially liked, she would stop for as long as her mind found pleasure grazing there' (Laurent 1936: 303). But Teresa weaves her text further, tying in practical advice, as when she compares the lack of disposition of a soul with eating disorders: 'y el alma descontenta es como quien tiene gran hastío, que por bueno que sea el manjar, le da en rostro; y cuando los sanos toman gran gusto en comer, le hace mayor asco en el estómago del que tiene hastío' (CE 20.2; 1986: 291) or when she warns against the dangers of gluttony to which the pleasurable experience of meditative prayer might lead: 'somos tan indiscretos que, como es pena suave y gustosa, nunca nos pensamos hartar de esta pena: comemos sin tasa, ayudamos como acá podemos a este deseo, y ansí algunas veces mata' (CE 32. 1; 1986: 316).

In sixteenth-century Spanish devotional writing, digestive imagery is used not so much to make the point that the writer must show his own genius, as with Petrarch and Erasmus, but as an illustration of how meditative prayer can be a process of assimilation, as it was for St Catherine and other Christian mystics. This is the sense it has in the *Libro de la oración y consideración* of 1554, by the Dominican Fray Luis de Granada:

> Porque así como dicen los médicos que para que las medicinas aprovechen, es menester que sean primero actuadas y digeridas en el estómago con el calor natural (porque de otra manera ninguna cosa aprovecharían), así también, para que los misterios de nuestra fe nos sean provechosos y saludables, conviene que sean primero actuados y digeridos en nuestro corazón con el calor de la devoción y meditación; porque de otra manera muy poco aprovecharán.
>
> (Luis de Granada 1855: II. 1)

Luis de Granada's books were amongst those specifically recommended by Teresa to her nuns in a passage of the *Constituciones*, where she also makes a comparison between spiritual nourishment and bodily nourishment:

> Tenga cuenta la Priora con que aya buenos libros, en especial *Cartuxanos*, *Flos Sanctorum*, *Contemptus Mundi*, *Oratorio de religiosos*, los de fray Luys de Granada, y los del padre fray Pedro de Alcántara: porque es en parte este mantenimiento tan necessario para el alma, como el comer para el cuerpo.[7]
>
> (*Constituciones* 10. 2; Teresa de Jesús 1978: 35 – 36)

The books Teresa recommends were indeed amongst the most popular devotional treatises at the time. Her comparison, 'necesario para el alma como el comer para el cuerpo', appears to be a well-assimilated idea, which could have been fed to her by Granada or by other popular preachers. Granada uses it to make himself understood by the common people: 'porque no hay más diferencia entre el sermón y la consideración, que entre la lición y consideración desta mesma lición, o que entre el manjar puesto en un plato, y él mesmo digerido y cocido en el estómago' (1855: II. 3). He makes it clear that he is writing for all Christians, lettered and unlettered, and he exhorts his readers and listeners to chew on the doctrinal ideas which he feeds them:

---

7.   This is the text of the facsimile edition of the printed version of 1581. Interestingly, the text of the oldest manuscript version does not include a mention of Granada: 'Tenga en cuenta la Priora con que haya buenos libros, en especial *Cartujanos*, *Flos Santorum*, *Contentus Mundi*, *Oratorio de religiosos*, los de fray Pedro de Alcántara, porque es en parte tan necesario este mantenimiento para el alma como el comer para el cuerpo' (*Constituciones*, 1. 13; see Teresa de Jesús 1986: 819 – 40 (821)). But Granada is mentioned again in the draft manuscript for the friars, also included in the BAC edition.

los cuales no se contentasen con comer las cosas de Dios, creyéndolas por
la fe, sino rumiándolas también después de comidas, por la consideración,
y escudriñando los misterios que creyeron, y entendiendo el tomo y la
grandeza dellos, repartiendo luego este manjar por todos los miembros
espirituales del ánima para sustentación y reparo della.

(1855: II. 2)

This kind of exhortation was considered to be dangerous by some of
Granada's fellow churchmen, who saw themselves as guarantors of the orthodoxy of Church doctrine and were consequently wary of individual interpretations of it. One of those guarantors, the Inquisitor-General Fernando de
Valdés, issued a decree condemning the books in Spanish which dealt with
prayer, fearing that they might contribute to the popularization of this practice. In fact, most of the books included in the *Index librorum prohibitorum*
published by Valdés in 1559 did not actually contain unsound doctrine, but
were simply regarded as dangerous because they were aimed at a wide audience not necessarily trained in theology and Latin. Thus, in his *Censura del
Catecismo cristiano de Carranza* (completed in 1563), Melchor Cano attacks
his fellow Dominican:

A fray Luis le podía la Iglesia reprender gravemente tres cosas. La una
en que pretendió hacer contemplativos y perfectos a todos, y enseñar al
pueblo en castellano lo que a pocos de él conviene; porque muy pocos
populares pretenderán ir a la perfección por aquel camino de fray Luis
que no se desbaraten en los ejercicios de la vida activa competentes a sus
estados. Y por el provecho de algunos pocos dar por escrito doctrina en
que muchos peligrarán por no tener fuerzas ni capacidad para ello, siempre se tuvo por indiscreción, perjudicial al bien público y contraria al seso
y prudencia de san Pablo, según al principio de estas censuras se dijo.

(Cano 1871: 597)

The Inquisitor Valdés judged that Granada's *Libro de la oración y consideración* addressed an entirely inappropriate audience, and he referred to this
book, without any apparent irony, as 'cosas de contemplación para mujeres de
carpinteros' (Luis de Granada 1908: 440–41).

Teresa's *Camino de perfección* could not but establish a dialogue with other
books on mental prayer. This was a risky enterprise, since most of the vernacular books dealing with the subject had been placed on the 1559 Index. Of
these she had most probably read Juan de Ávila's *Audi, filia*, Luis de
Granada's *Libro de la oración y consideración*, Bernabé de Palma's *Via spiritus*

and Francisco de Hevia's *Itinerario de la oración*, although she does not dare to refer to any of these titles.[8] *Camino* itself, had it been printed, would have seemed a good candidate for inclusion on such an Index. It is thus not surprising that in its first version she addresses a very specific audience within the protective convent walls.

Teresa offers her book to the nuns as the book which can meet their need for spiritual guidance. If they are to be deprived of other books, the one Teresa is writing for them will be sufficient if they study it carefully:

> Y ansí me ha parecido (pues como digo, hablo con almas que no pueden ansí recogerse en otros misterios – que les parece son artificios – y algunos ingenios tan ingeniosos que nada les contenta) iré fundando por aquí unos principios y medios y fines de oración – aunque en cosas tan subidas no haré sino tocar, porque, como digo, las tengo ya escritas – ; y no os podrán quitar libro, que no os quede tan buen libro; que si sois estudiosas con humildad, no havéis menester otra cosa.
>
> (CE 35. 4; 1986: 324)

Camino will be sufficient only up to a point. More advanced learners are referred to the *Vida*, where she has dealt more thoroughly with the higher stages of prayer ('ya las tengo escritas').

---

8. Of these the only book she mentions at all in her writing is Granada's, as we saw above. Apart from the passage of *Constituciones* in which she mentions book titles, we only have evidence of her reading in parts of *Vida*, where she mentions having read Osuna's *Tercer abecedario* (*Vida* 4. 6), Laredo's *Subida del Monte Sión* (*Vida* 23. 12), and the Spanish version (1502 – 03) of Ludolph of Saxony's *Vita Christi* (*Vida* 38. 9). In *Camino* there is a complete absence of titles, combined with an obsessive mention of books and writings, taken as a generic category: 'porque hay tanto escrito de esta virtud' (CE 2. 7; CV 2. 7); 'si en otros libros tan menudamente lo hallardes escrito' (CE 6. 8; slightly altered in CV 4. 11); 'hay tantos libros escritos y tan buenos y de personas tales' (CE 30. 1; CV 19. 1); 'ni eran menester otros libros' (CE 35. 3; CV 21. 3); 'algunas veces con tantos libros parece que se nos pierde la devoción' (CE 35. 4; altered in CV 21. 4); 'también es gran remedio tomar un buen libro de romance' (CE 43. 3; altered in CV 26. 10)'; 'como está escrito en algunos libros ... los que escriven oración mental' (CE 49. 4; altered in CV 29. 5). It is also interesting that most of these references are omitted in the second version of *Camino* 'aunque no en todos los santos que escrivieron, u muchos' (CE 13. 2; omitted from CV 9. 2); 'en muchas partes, como he dicho, lo hallaréis escrito; en todos los más libros no se trata otra cosa sino cuán bueno es huir del mundo' (CE 13. 4; omitted from CV 9. 4); 'que hartos libros tenéis que os las enseñan' (CE 24. 3; whole chapter omitted in CV); 'y otros muchos que saben lo que escriven' (CE 24 .3); 'porque esto se sabe ya muy sabido y lo han escrito muchos' (CE 29. 6; omitted from CV 18. 8); 'que lo he leído' (CE 31. 2; omitted from CV 19. 5); 'y aunque en algún libro he leído lo bien que es llevar este principio, y aun en algunos' (CE 35. 2; omitted from CV 21. 2); 'y en otros libros están dichas algunas' (CE 39. 1; omitted from CV 23. 1).

The impact of Valdés's prohibition was still alive when Teresa insisted that she herself did not like to read books whose authors were not entirely approved of:

> Siempre yo he sido aficionada y me han recogido más las palabras de los Evangelios que se salieron por aquella sacratísima boca ansí como las decía, que libros muy bien concertados; en especial si no era el autor muy aprovado, no los havía gana de leer.

(CE 35. 4; 1986: 324)

Which 'suspect' authors Teresa was referring to cannot be known. What was important for her to emphasize was that she had dismissed the books of learned men in favour of words from the Gospels, which were written by men, but whose author was God: 'que se salieron por aquella sacratísima boca ansí como las decía'.

We know, nevertheless, that Teresa no longer had direct access to the text of the Gospels, since all Spanish translations had been banned by the 1559 Index. The situation had been further complicated by the importance attached to Cano's *Censura del Catecismo cristiano de Carranza*, and the ideas woven into it, as for example: 'por más que las mujeres reclamen con insaçiable apetito comer de este fruto [the reading of the Scriptures], es necesario vedarlo y poner cuchillo de fuego para que el pueblo no llegue a él' (1871: 597).[9] Unable to eat the fruit of the Book of Books, Teresa was still fed small pieces of the Gospels through sermons and through the passages from the Life of Christ which were interwoven in popular devotional texts such as Ludolph of Saxony's *Vita Christi*. Only through a complex network of nourishing intertexts could Teresa have been able to taste the words she believed were said by God.

ELENA CARRERA

Trinity College, Oxford

---

9.   Despite Cano's prohibition, however, Teresa embarked on an interpretation of one of the Psalms in her first manuscript of *Camino* (CE 31. 2; 1986: 314). It is hardly surprising that the censor García de Toledo should have followed Cano's recommendation and crossed out the entire passage, writing in the margin: 'no es éste el sentido aclaratorio del psalmo'. The passage was omitted in the second version of *Camino* (CV 19. 3).

'LAS LETRAS Y LAS ARMAS':
FICTIONAL PLEASURE AND POWER
IN MARÍA DE ZAYAS'S
'TARDE LLEGA EL DESENGAÑO'

MARÍA DE ZAYAS'S SHORT STORIES have been the subject of a growing body of criticism in the wake of the feminist opening up of the debate on fiction written by women in the seventeenth century. Perhaps predictably, when judged by twentieth-century standards Zayas is frequently found wanting by critics who perceive her writings to be conservative, ambiguous in their feminist message, or grounded in masculine discourse. According to Alicia Yllera, Zayas 'trata el tema [del femenismo] con unos presupuestos mucho más conservadores de lo que a primera vista podría parecer' (Zayas 1983: 49). Lou Charnon-Deutsch mentions the 'ambiguities of her stories of female victimization and female agency' and concludes that, whatever the virtues of the tales, they 'are still stories of sexual difference' (1991: 16, 26). Indeed, implicit throughout Charnon-Deutsch's article is her disappointment that Zayas's narrative suffers the consequences of masculine discourse. Paul Julian Smith writes that Zayas 'cannot transcend the phallocratic logic of her own time' (1989: 31). Other commentators, far from being perplexed by what critics might deem to be Zayas's ambivalent standpoint, see her texts as centred on groupings of fixed binary oppositions. Marcia Welles, for example (1978: 307), considers 'antithetical feminine archetypes' and, in the case of Zayas, differentiates female characters by placing them in categories which she terms the negative feminine (for example, sorceress, seductress, wicked older woman) and the positive feminine (virginal figure, the woman who enters the convent). She also sets up a textual opposition between 'sensual and intellectual love' (308), and asserts that 'the constancy of this binary opposition in the tales establishes it as an essential structure pattern as well as a thematic core of the spiritual reality of their significance' (307). Sandra Foa,

following José Antonio Maravall, sees Zayas's tales as characterized by conflict between men and women (1978: 129). Riera and Cotoner categorize the
women in Zayas's novels and fit them into three fundamental sets of oppositions: passive/active; ingenuous-ignorant/cynical-astute-experienced; and
voluntarist/ possibilist (*sic*) (1987: 150). This type of interpretation would
seem to serve little other purpose than that of rewriting the stories in discourses of patriarchy and thereby sustaining paradigms of inequality and
domination within the text, and they would suggest that María de Zayas, for
all the apparent outspokenness of her ideas on women, is none the less
obliged in the end to conform to the female norm set out in the literary conventions within which she is writing.

What I propose to do, through a reading of 'Tarde llega el desengaño', the
fourth of the stories in *Desengaños amorosos* (1647), is to re-evaluate Zayas's
story in order to show how the *Desengaños amorosos* stress the female narrators, since the separate tales in the collection are told by women rather than
by men, who are assigned the role of audience. In the context of 'Tarde llega
el desengaño', the narrator Filis has the advantage of the character Don
Martín, in that she controls the development of the tale whilst he takes up a
place as the passive audience of the events and the object of the moral lesson
contained in them. The tale can be understood, then, as an indictment not of
the victimization of women by Don Jaime (which might be the reading of a
female audience) but of his foolishness in misjudging the actions and intentions of powerful women figures who contrive to destroy him: in other
words, as a chastening lesson for a male audience. At the same time, it can be
read as putting into practice female powers in fiction. I also wish to suggest
ways in which the central section of the tale stands independently as a depiction of female pleasure and power at the heart of the narrative through an unconventional reworking of other source tales which found their first literary
expression in Apuleius's *Golden Ass*. In sum, I shall assert that 'Tarde llega el
desengaño' need not be read as a shifting sand of indecision on the part of the
author, nor as an impasse blocked by the limitations of patriarchal discourse,
nor as the embodiment of fixed codes of female depravity or passivity. Instead, it can be seen as a tale of the multiple and simultaneous possibilities for
those fictional women who control, in Filis's words, 'las letras y las armas'
(Zayas 1983: 231), and as a fantasy of female power and female autonomy.

'Tarde llega el desengaño' is one of a series of tales told by a group of friends to entertain Lisis, who is recovering from a bout of quartan fever, whilst she is awaiting her marriage to Don Diego. The synopsis of the chapter entitled 'Desengaño cuarto' is as follows. Filis, one of Lisis's circle of friends, prefaces her narrative with a diatribe in defence of women, advocating that, in defiance of the limitations imposed upon their sex, they resort to both 'las letras y las armas' (Zayas 1983: 231) in order to assert themselves against men in society. She then tells the tale of Don Martín, young and in love, who is shipwrecked on Gran Canaria. There he is befriended and given lodgings by Don Jaime de Aragón, a nobleman who lives in a bizarre domestic set-up: a beautiful, starving girl is kept prisoner in a cell and forced to drink from a skull, whilst an ugly black woman dressed in finery dines at his table. Prompted by his guests' bewilderment, Don Jaime tells his own story. First, he recounts a youthful adventure in Flanders, where he submits, blindfolded, to being taken to visit a mysterious nameless woman who, having enjoyed his sexual services in a pitch-black room, showers him with money and stipulates that he should not reveal their liaison. He returns nightly for more of the same, until a friend named Baltasar, growing curious about his lavish lifestyle, persuades him to discover the identity of the mysterious woman and betray her. She turns out to be an extraordinary beauty and heiress called Lucrecia but, when she realizes that Don Jaime has divulged their secret relationship, she gives orders to have him killed. He narrowly escapes death, and retires for his own safety to the Canaries. He is obsessed by his lost love, Lucrecia, but eventually meets a woman who is her image, and marries her. This woman is Elena, the beautiful prisoner. The reason for her punishment is that, after his return from a short trip, Don Jaime is told by Elena's negro slave that Elena and her cousin have been indulging in illicit sexual relations. In fury, Don Jaime has the cousin burned alive, but keeps his skull as a drinking vessel for Elena, who is condemned to humiliation and starvation. Don Martín has his doubts about the situation which has been explained to him, but retires to bed. Almost immediately, the slave woman, who is dying, wakes the the household with her confession that she framed Elena and the cousin because of a personal grudge. Don Jaime finishes the slave off with his dagger, but when Elena's cell is unlocked, it transpires that she has already died an angelic death. Don Jaime is beside himself with grief, and Don Martín, much chastened by these events, returns home to lead an exemplary married life. Lisis's assembled guests express their admiration for Elena's lengthy suffering, and adjourn for dinner.

In order to appreciate what María de Zayas is doing in this story, it has to be read as a whole, which critics invariably choose not to do, preferring instead to concentrate on discrete sections of the text. Filis's diatribe which prefaces the story is, quite rightly, produced as evidence of Zayas's feminist manifesto (Zayas 1983: 50). Juan Goytisolo concentrates on the erotic dimensions of the story as supplied in the central episode about the mysterious Lucrecia (1977: 100–01). The final section of the tale is chiefly adduced as an example of the appalling and gratuitous cruelty meted out by men to women, and their passivity in succumbing to it: 'encontramos el ejemplo más flagrante de pasividad en Doña Elena, a lo largo de todas las vejaciones de las que llega a ser objeto' (Riera & Cotoner 1987: 157). Undoubtedly, one reason for the focus on the elements which form the tale, rather than on the tale as a whole, is that for a modern readership a story of this kind raises considerable problems of interpretation. It is on its surface both rambling and disconnected, with little logical progression between the episodes: the narrative is sustained, as are so many stories of the time, by peripeteia, by the forward movement of Don Jaime as his passage through life propels him from Spain to Flanders to Gran Canaria, and also by the parallel of the journeys of Don Martín from Flanders to Gran Canaria to Spain. The meaning of the successive narrations is to a large extent deferred: there is no sustained link, for example, between the episode involving Lucrecia and that which centres on Elena, save that Elena is the living image of Lucrecia and for this reason Don Jaime elects to marry her. No cause and effect is ever posited for Don Jaime's experience with the first woman and his treatment of the second. Furthermore, whilst Zayas's views on the condition of women as articulated by Filis seem clear, they do not square with the frankly unhelpful binary oppositions which are set up beween Lucrecia as seductress and Elena as innocent angel, between Elena as victim and the negro slave as vengeful persecutor.

A reading of the tale as a whole, however, sheds new light on its importance as a female-centred narrative written by a female, and on the structural and thematic importance of the diverse elements which it comprises. Referring to the *Desengaños* collection, Maroto Camino mentions how the 'layer of narrators deployed by Zayas within the frame provides an interesting pattern' (1994: 522). This applies particularly to 'Tarde llega el desengaño' in which the layers of narrative indicate the multiplicity of female roles within and without the text: Zayas herself, as author; Filis, the narrator of the fiction; the characters in her fiction – the powerful, independent, sexual Lucrecia; the honest, pure and victimized Elena; and the treacherous slave woman – and, finally, the historical women who are eulogized in Filis's introductory diatribe: princesses and queens who hold political power; nuns, poets and dramatists who influence cultural developments. Filis's comments are pertinent in elucidating the importance to women of 'las letras y las armas' in their struggle against the men who deprive them of social power and influence:

> De manera que no voy fuera de camino en que los hombres de temor y envidia las privan [a las mujeres] de las letras y las armas, como hacen los moros a los cristianos que han de servir donde hay mujeres, que los hacen eunucos por estar seguros de ellos. ¡Ah, damas hermosas, qué os pudiera decir, si supiera que como soy oída no había de ser murmurada! ¡Ea, dejemos las galas, rosas y rizos, y volvamos por nosotras: unas, con el entendimiento, y otras, con las armas!
>
> (Zayas 1983: 231)

Amy Williamsen notes that 'in the *Desengaños*, men are excluded from the act of narration – they are relegated to the role of narratees. The textual description of the organization of the "sarao" states that it constitutes the woman's usurpation of a previously male-dominated sphere' (1991: 643). This observation relates in microcosm to 'Tarde llega el desengaño': Don Jaime's story is mediated by the female voice, which at the same time sets Don Martín up as the nominal protagonist of the frame story and as the passive and horrified witness of Elena's degradation and the killing of the slave woman. Thus Don Jaime is presented as a victim of his own foolishness in attempting to betray Lucrecia and in believing the dishonest slave, whilst the 'escarmentado en el suceso que vio por sus ojos' (Zayas 1983: 254) of the piece is Don Martín, who is patently moved by Don Jaime's circumstances as they unfold. This subverts the usual critical assumption that a tale such as this, written apparently within a conventional framework, is intended to be heard or read by a female audience (and presumably a male one as well) as outlawing female sexual insatiability and treachery, or prescribing submission to the punishments meted out by men. Instead, it is upon the male protagonists that the effects of misguided behaviour and the effects of the text are seen, and the active woman narrator or protagonist is set against the passive male audience or character who is acted upon.

Filis's comments on the need to have recourse to 'las letras y las armas' refer to her own powers in narrating fiction as outlined above, and to her pleasure in the manipulation of the text, as well as on another plane to Lucrecia's
ability to generate the situation in which Don Jaime finds himself and, in effect, to become the prime mover of their story. The central section of the tale,
the Lucrecia episode, is frequently passed over by critics. Yet, by virtue of its
centrality, and the fact that it stands furthest back in time and can therefore
be seen as lying at the origin of the events which occur, it is also the section
which merits closest attention. It can be read as a narrative of female power
and of female pleasure, and therefore ties back into Filis's arguments about
'las letras y las armas' in the opening paragraphs, and forward into the later
episode when the slave woman fashions a role for herself as Don Jaime's wife
by creating a fiction about Elena upon which he acts. Lucrecia creates the
conditions for her own pleasure and power, through the seduction and later
the attempted murder of Don Jaime, and does so by generating a sequence of
events which, initially at least, defies his interpretation, and prevents him from
reading her intentions. From within her shuttered rooms, Lucrecia moves a
whole world of shadowy messengers and henchmen. To reach her, Don Jaime
is carried for over an hour on horseback through a maze of streets, which represents the peripeteia of the narrative which is engineered by Lucrecia, although it finally transpires that this progression is an illusion, a fiction, since
Lucrecia's house is in fact at a short distance from his own and the journey is
merely a subterfuge to confuse him. Don Jaime is blindfolded and able to
make sense of where he is only through indirect signs – the rustle of Lucrecia's
silk dress, the scent of her apartments – and he deciphers her body only with
his hands: 'esta mano que tengo en la mía no puede ser sino la de un ángel',
'empecé a procurar por el tiento a conocer lo que la vista no podía' (Zayas
1983: 241). In his imagination, another level of fiction is generated, the image
of Lucrecia as 'ángel' or 'deidad' (241). Once Don Jaime demands and is
granted sight of Lucrecia, the image created slips from his grasp: 'Mira lo que
haces', warns Lucrecia (244), but the man who now sees is metaphorically
blind, unable to comprehend and act upon her meaning. Lucrecia's power
over Don Jaime long outlives the scars of the failed attempt to murder him,
for he carries with him the image of Lucrecia, the fiction which takes root as
an obsession in his mind: 'aún vivía en mi alma la imagen adorada de ma-

dama Lucrecia, perdida el mismo día que la vi; que aunque había sido causa de tanto mal como padecí, no la podía olvidar ni aborrecer' (246–47).

It is worthy of note that Lisis's guests, although quick to draw a moral from the situation of Don Jaime and Elena, make no comment on the behaviour of Lucrecia. This gap in the text may be no more than that, but it is also possible that this omission is a tacit approval of the actions of Lucrecia in seducing and punishing the object of her desire. The erotic or sexual content of María de Zayas's stories disgusted nineteenth-century critics who, perversely, did not hesitate to make the most of it. George Ticknor judged her work some of 'the filthiest and most immodest I have ever read' (Maroto Camino 1994: 521), whilst Pfandl talks about 'una libertina enumeración de diversas aventuras de amor de un realismo extraviado... que con demasiada frecuencia degenera unas veces en lo terrible y perverso y otras en obscena liviandad' (Goytisolo 1977: 88). Recent critics, despite their more permissive tone, are not exempt from interpreting María de Zayas's sexually charged women characters from within the discourse of male prejudice about such women, or seeing their behaviour as a mere inversion of male sexuality. So, Charnon-Deutsch uses the loaded words 'sexual predators' (1991: 24) to describe these women, Paul Julian Smith sees them 'permitted to adopt a travesty of man' (1989: 33), and for Goytisolo 'la protagonista se viriliza' (1977: 100). As Mercedes Maroto Camino points out, 'Goytisolo's "disidencia" is informed by the misogynist topos of the sexual insatiability of women and the consequent emasculation of men' (1994: 522).

In point of fact, María de Zayas's depiction of the relationship of Lucrecia and Don Jaime, and hence, at least in part, its supposedly lascivious content and the presentation of sexual roles within it, owes much to the folk-tale and to the literary traditions which lie behind it. The precise nature of this intertextual debt can only tentatively be suggested, and it is my intention to do so merely in order to illuminate the way in which Zayas transforms the characters and scenarios which she has culled from her reading at the same time as she demonstrates the transformations –for better or worse– which are brought about by love or lust.

Among the possible sources for this episode suggested by Edwin Place is Céspedes y Meneses's *Varia fortuna del soldado Píndaro*, which was first published in 1626 (Place 1923: 42–43). In significant respects *El soldado Píndaro* indeed carries the germ of Zayas's Lucrecia episode. A veiled woman accosts

Píndaro from within her sedan chair and declares herself to him. She asks
him to be discreet: 'Mi claridad y estado piden, señor, en su resguardo la
misma confiança' (Céspedes y Meneses 1975: 15). A month later, the love-
lorn woman sends for Píndaro, who is carried 'un grande espacio' (24) in a
closed sedan chair and shown up to her lodgings (which later turn out to be on
the floor above his own), where he notes (as Don Jaime will do later) 'la fra-
gancia y olor del aposento' (24). The woman enters in half-light so that Píndaro cannot see her clearly. Overcome by his presence, she swoons, and her
servant rushes in to help, carrying a lantern which permits Píndaro to see her.
He leaves, sworn to secrecy and hopelessly in love. The relationship develops
but fails when the woman realizes that Píndaro has revealed the affair to his
brother, and after she sees him out in the company of his friends, fears that
they too may be aware of the situation. She lures Píndaro to her apartments,
where he is attacked by three hired assassins, but escapes with his life. By this
time, Píndaro is aware that his mistress is in fact the estranged wife of a nobleman, and the episode ends with his removal to Madrid after a bitter invec-
tive against women and their failings: '¡O quántos son los daños y los males
que an visto sobre sí el mundo y los hombres por su causa!' (50). By far the
greater part of the Céspedes y Meneses episode, however, is devoted to the
tedious unfolding of the affair, consisting of the woman's haranguing of Píndaro for his bad behaviour, the exchange of conventional love letters, long
separations, incidental incidents, and so forth, and the urgency and terseness
of Zayas's writing – not to mention her presentation of the woman involved in
a favourable light – is nowhere to be found. The female protagonist is entirely
subordinated to the first-person eponymous narrator (whose account is not
framed by other narrative voices, as occurs in 'Tarde llega el desengaño') and
merely serves as a means to the end of warning against women with which
Píndaro rounds off his adventure.

To what extent Zayas may have taken the outlines of her story from Céspedes y Meneses cannot be ascertained. What does seem likely, however, is
that both Céspedes y Meneses and Zayas were working from common
sources. In her edition of the *Desengaños amorosos*, Alicia Yllera mentions
the general indebtedness of the Renaissance novella to Apuleius's *Golden Ass*
and in particular to the story of Cupid and Psyche (Zayas 1983: 23). It is not
inconceivable that, in *El soldado Píndaro*, Céspedes y Meneses is loosely indebted to Apuleius. As we shall see, Cervantes almost certainly drew on the

Cupid and Psyche tale and its frame story of the lovers Charites and Tlepole-mus for an episode in *Los trabajos de Persiles y Sigismunda* (1617). Zayas may have known both these and other contemporary versions of tales deriving from *The Golden Ass*, but her handling of sexual behaviour and gender roles in 'Tarde llega el desengaño' also suggests an independent debt to Apuleius.

The tale of Cupid and Psyche would have been familiar to sixteenth and early seventeenth-century readers through Diego López de Cortegana's translation of *The Golden Ass*, entitled *Metamorfosis, o El asno de oro*, which was first printed in either 1513 or 1525 and ran through seven later editions, the last of them printed in Seville in 1613 (Apuleius 1988: 26). In his introduction to a recent edition, García Gual admits the difficulties of calibrating the influence of such works on the development of Spanish prose fiction, but notes that 'modifican el panorama literario nacional, como lo hizo ésta de modo claro' (29). He insists that this translation 'trajo consigo una no-table ampliación del horizonte de expectativas de nuestra literatura' (30), and relates its impact on later writings to the central theme of transformation, and to 'su atmósfera realista y, a la par, fantástica... su erotismo, su truculencia, su ácido humor' (31).

Apuleius's tale of Cupid and Psyche is presented as follows in *El asno de oro* (Apuleius 1988: 143–88). Psyche, a beautiful young girl, becomes an object of rivalry for Venus, who in her jealousy orders Cupid to marry the girl off to a monster. Smitten with love for Psyche, Cupid carries her off and makes her his wife but, although she lives surrounded by splendour and luxury, she is never granted sight of her husband, who lays this down as the condition of the continuation of their marriage. Psyche's two sisters grow jealous of her good fortune, and persuade her to discover the identity of her husband who, they tell her, is indeed a monster. One night, Psyche brings out an oil lamp and has a knife at the ready to kill her husband as he sleeps. As soon as she sees him, however, she is overcome by his beauty, and when she pricks her finger on one of his arrows, falls deeply in love with him. A drop of burning oil falls on Cupid and awakens him; he flies away and Psyche is cast out into the world in search of her lost husband. After many trials they are happily reunited. The frame story within which the tale of Cupid and Psyche is set, and which is equally important in providing a model for Spanish authors, has a rather different ending (Apuleius 1988: 217–28). Charites marries Tlepolemus, but a jealous former suitor, Thrasyllus, organizes a hunting trip in the course of

which he kills Tlepolemus, disguising the murder as the attack of a wild boar.
Charites is grief-stricken, but when Thrasyllus begins to court her less than a
month afterwards, she has a dream in which her husband returns to divulge
the truth of his murder. She wreaks vengeance on Thrasyllus by luring him to
her chamber with a promise of sexual fulfilment, drugging him with a sleeping
draught, and putting his eyes out with a hairpin. She then commits suicide
and Thrasyllus, upon waking, is so aghast at the tragedy which he has brought
about that he entombs himself alive.

A convincing account of the processes of intertextual transformation at
work in the seventeenth century is given by Diana de Armas Wilson (1994).
In an article entitled 'Homage to Apuleius: Cervantes' Avenging Psyche', she
analyses the sources and function of the interpolated tale of the Countess Ruperta which occurs towards the end of *Los trabajos de Persiles y Sigismunda*
(Cervantes 1969: 384–92), and which draws closely on Apuleius's tale of Cupid and Psyche and on the frame tale of Charites and Tlepolemus. The background to the Countess Ruperta story is told to Periandro (Persiles), Auristela
(Sigismunda), and the assembled company by an old man, who recounts how
the Countess's husband was murdered by a nobleman who at one time had
aspired to be her suitor. Since then, she has travelled Europe with her husband's skull and his bloodied shirt, plotting revenge. The onlookers are allowed to spy on Ruperta in her bedroom as the presence of Croriano, the son
of the murderer, is announced to her. She waits until night and enters Croriano's room holding a lantern and armed with a knife, but is overcome by his
beauty and instead of killing him, she seduces him. Wilson demonstrates how
Cervantes, using elements of the Cupid and Psyche tale, but basing himself
chiefly on the Charites and Tlepolemus story, transforms his model in such a
way that 'Apuleius's harrowing revenge narrative of Charites and Tlepolemus
is hollowed out, transmuted into a comic romance, a tale of countesses and
Cupids that closes with a merry, if hugger-mugger, pre-Tridentine wedding'
(1994: 97). She comments on the conventional misogynistic attitudes which
already exist in *The Golden Ass*, and which are amplified in Cervantes's reworking of the material when the events recounted and witnessed are 'framed'
by a misogynist voice (90), as the narrator permits himself a series of asides on
the anger of women: 'Que la cólera de la mujer no tiene límite' (Cervantes
1969: 386); '¿Qué no hace una mujer enojada?' (389); and Ruperta's servant
is heard to complain of the inconstancy of women: 'Murmuró de la facilidad

de Ruperta, y en general, de todas las mujeres, y el menor vituperio que dellas dijo fue llamarlas antojadizas' (392). Wilson also considers Cervantes's tongue-in-cheek treatment of the reversal of gender roles, when Ruperta becomes the 'hyper-masculinized heroine' akin to Psyche who 'undergoes a sex change' in Apuleius's original when she is on the point of killing Cupid, whilst Croriano is described as having the properties of the female Medusa (1994: 92). What she concludes, then, is that Cervantes succeeds in humorously transforming or debunking the source text which he manipulates, and subverting assumptions about gender, just as he transforms the roles of his female and male characters, and turns the scenario of vengeance provided by Apuleius into a comic happy ending.

Wilson also points out that Cervantes succeeds in avoiding the salacious content of Apuleius's text, which would have been offensive to the literary sensibilities of the seventeenth century (1994: 90). The only significant difference between the amorous encounters of Ruperta and her lover Croriano and those of Lucrecia and Don Jaime lies in the fact that Ruperta and Croriano see their sexual activities sanctioned by witnesses to their 'marriage' (Cervantes 1969: 391), whereas Lucrecia insists that Don Jaime keep their trysts a secret (Zayas 1983: 241), although she later intimates that her intentions towards Don Jaime are honourable and that she hopes eventually to marry him: 'aunque me salen muchos casamientos, ninguno acepto ni aceptaré hasta que el Cielo me dé lugar para hacerte mi esposo' (244). The attitude of both women protagonists to the sexual liaison is in fact similarly robust, since both are struck with lust at the sight of their lovers, suggesting that, notwithstanding a particular wish to depict her woman protagonist as a sexual being, Zayas was indeed working within the accepted norms of contemporary literature:

> [Ruperta] vio... la belleza de Croriano... y en un instante no le escogió para víctima de su cruel sacrificio, sino para holocausto santo de su gusto. –¡Ay! –dijo entre sí–, generoso mancebo, y ¡cuán mejor eres tú para ser mi esposo que para ser objeto de mi venganza!
>
> (Cervantes 1969: 389)

> No juzgues a desenvoltura esto que has visto, sino a fuerza de amor, de que he querido muchas veces librarme... mas tu gala y bizarría han podido más.
>
> (Zayas 1983: 241)

It can be argued that María de Zayas, in similar fashion to Cervantes, has re-
worked the two familiar stories and transformed them, producing in Wilson's
words 'a metamorphosis of the *Metamorphoses* [i.e. *The Golden Ass*]' (1994:
94), which serves her own purposes in writing the *Desengaños*. Zayas may be
directly indebted to the vernacular translation of Apuleius or may in fact be
adapting Cervantes's tale of the Countess Ruperta, the Céspedes y Meneses
story of *El soldado Píndaro*, or perhaps some other tale based on Apuleius.
Whatever the case, the direct parallels and contrasts with the interpolated stories in Cortegana's translation of *El asno de oro* are clear, and do not always
coincide with details given in the Céspedes y Meneses or Cervantes texts.
From the Psyche and Cupid tale, Zayas picks up and adapts or subverts several features. The most obvious of these is the central relationship in which
the dominant partner enjoins the lover not to seek to discover his identity.
Since the dominant partner is the woman Lucrecia, and the perplexed lover
the man, Don Jaime, Zayas has incorporated the role reversal which is suggested by Apuleius when Psyche decides to kill her husband, and used as a device by Céspedes y Meneses and by Cervantes to enable the Countess Ruperta
to pursue her revenge (Wilson 1994: 92). Lucrecia warns Don Jaime not to
seek to see her: 'que no nos convenía, porque verla y perderla había de ser
uno' (Zayas 1983: 242), echoing both the warnings given to Psyche in the
López de Cortegana translation not to 'buscar ni saber el gesto y figura de su
marido, por que, con esta sacrílega curiosidad, no caiga de tanta riqueza y
bienaventuranza como tiene: que haciéndola de otra manera, jamás le vería
ni tocaría' (Apuleius 1988: 153), and also Cupid's admonishment that, should
Psyche seek to see his face, 'como muchas veces te he dicho, tú no la verás
más, si la ves' (157). Although it is Lucrecia who provides the candle which
reveals her face to Don Jaime, the discovery corresponds with Psyche's first
sight of Cupid: 'saliendo entre sus hermosos dedos con una bujía de cera en-
cendida vi, no una mujer, sino un serafín' (Zayas 1983: 244); 'Como ella
alumbrase con el candil... vido una bestia, la más mansa y dulcísima de todas
las fieras: digo que era aquel hermoso dios del amor que se llama Cupido'
(Apuleius 1988: 163–64). Lucrecia tries to keep Don Jaime quiet by giving
him gifts and money which correspond to the luxury of Psyche's life as Cupid's
wife: 'sin faltar... ella de colmarme de dineros y preciosas joyas... con que
yo me trataba como un príncipe' (Zayas 1983: 242).

The two envious sisters who persuade Psyche to unmask her husband are transformed in 'Tarde llega el desengaño' into the figure of Don Baltasar, who urges Don Jaime to reveal the secret of his night-time absences and new-found riches, and when Don Jaime betrays Lucrecia he finds himself, like Psyche, wandering the world in search of his lost love: 'me puse en camino... no tenía ninguna voluntad de casarme, porque aún vivía en mi alma la imagen adorada de madama Lucrecia, perdida el mismo día que la vi' (246 – 47); 'Psiche... solamente adorando su deidad, comenzó a andar su camino' (Apuleius 1988: 167). As with Cervantes's adaptation of Apuleius, Zayas leaves aside the elements of the tale which are not useful to her purpose, namely the allegorical possibilities of the story and the happy ending (Wilson 1994: 94). In the manner of Cervantes, Zayas also blends in elements from Apuleius's tale of Charites and Tlepolemus. Like Charites, Lucrecia is a widow – 'viuda, mas muy moza, por haberla casado niña' (Zayas 1983: 244) – a fact which empowers her according to seventeenth-century convention to make her sexual advances to Don Jaime, just as Charites's luring of Thrasyllus with sexual favours is made possible thanks to her status as a widow in the original Apuleius. Furthermore, like Charites, and like the Countess Ruperta, Lucrecia sets out to wreak revenge: 'aún no estaba vengada [Lucrecia]... de mano de una mujer se había todo originado' (Zayas 1983: 246). In Lucrecia's case, of course, the revenge which she seeks is not upon a guilty third party, but upon the object of her desires, Don Jaime: 'esta noche te han de matar por mandado de quien más te quiere' (245), a statement which again echoes Psyche's attempt to kill Cupid.

However, whilst Cervantes adapts Apuleius in comic and romantic vein, the tone of the Lucrecia episode in 'Tarde llega el desengaño' magnifies the erotic and violent content present in the Cupid and Psyche and Charites and Tlepolemus tales in *El asno de oro* since, in Zayas's narrative, lust and revenge are ends in themselves and do not reach any ultimate resolution in marriage or death. What Zayas achieves, then, in the central section of 'Tarde llega el desengaño' is the subverting of Apuleius's tales, perhaps suggested by Céspedes y Meneses's and Cervantes's reworkings of the same material, in order to illuminate the power of the woman protagonist over the male lover – a power which compares later with the hold which the female slave exerts over her master.

Although she superficially adopts the same reversal of gender roles as is seen in Apuleius, Céspedes y Meneses, and Cervantes, the Lucrecia episode differs fundamentally from the other tales with their misogynistic frame narratives, in that it is enclosed within two female narratives, those of Zayas and Filis. On the wider level of the *Desengaños amorosos* collection, this successful engendering of narrative – despite their gender limitations – on the part of Lucrecia and the woman slave reflects back clearly on Filis's designs for women, which in turn shed light on Zayas's own narrative aims. Rather than being limited by the patriarchal discourse of her models, she shapes it according to her own ideal of deploying both 'las letras y las armas', demonstrating in the act of writing, as well as in the content of what is written, the possibilities for women as the generators and manipulators of fiction.[1]

JUDITH DRINKWATER

University of Leeds

---

1.   Since preparing this article, a further study has come to my attention. Frederick Alfred de Armas, *The Invisible Mistress: Aspects of Feminism and Fantasy in the Golden Age*, Biblioteca Siglo de Oro 2 (Charlottesville VA: Biblioteca Siglo de Oro, 1976) examines the reworkings and subversions of the Cupid and Psyche myth in a number of plays and *novelle*. He looks in particular at Masuccio's twenty-sixth *novella* as a possible source of the motif of the mysterious seductress in seventeenth-century Spain, as well as at Bandello's twenty-fifth *novella*, itself adapted from Masuccio. He considers the Lucrecia episode in Zayas's 'Tarde llega el desengaño' to be a 'version of Masuccio's *novella*' (31) and to be indebted to Céspedes y Meneses's *El soldado Píndaro*.

WOMEN WRITERS IN THE HISPANIC NOVEL CANON IN THE UNITED STATES

THE CENTRAL QUESTION of this paper is 'What is our contemporary novel canon, and which women writers and which texts written by women are in it?'[1] The answers – and also the questions – that we have discovered are based on the findings of a study that attempts to describe our current canon for contemporary Hispanic literature. We attempted to describe our current canon in the field of the contemporary novel of Spain and Spanish America, through an analysis of the principal pedagogical source used at most institutions of higher learning in the United States: graduate reading-lists. These lists are compiled by graduate faculties and distributed to graduate students. Students are usually examined on the works listed, and passing this examination is one requirement for the advanced degree. Although both the Spanish and Spanish-American reading-list canon have been reported (Brown & Johnson 1995), this paper focuses almost exclusively on peninsular writers, for reasons that will become clear.

In the first portion of this paper we describe the methods and results of our study, and outline our findings. In the second, we present new information about the proportional representation of peninsular and Hispanic-American writers in the individual reading-lists for the contemporary novel. The last part of this paper analyses distinct characteristics of the few contemporary texts written by women that have gained admission to the canon, and offers a hypothesis about the entrance requirements these texts have fulfilled. Our hope is that this 'state of the canon' report will serve as the basis for debate in the field of contemporary Hispanic studies, and that other suggested explanations for these findings will be advanced.

*   *   *   *   *

---

1.   For another version of this paper, which does not focus on women writers, see Brown & Johnson (1995).

DATA FOR THIS characterization of our literary canon were derived from the recent graduate reading lists of fifty-eight Spanish faculties in the Unites States that award doctorates. To obtain these lists, we contacted the Spanish departments or sections of seventy-four US universities that are leaders in Spanish graduate education. Selections were based on rankings of US graduate schools. The seventy-four institutions include the top-ranked forty graduate programmes in Spanish on the listing prepared by Gourman, and sixty-three of the graduate programmes in Spanish listed in *Peterson's Guide*. Universities from every region of the United States were included: twenty-five from the North-east, nine from the Mid-west, seven from the West Coast, four from the Rocky Mountain Region, eight from the South Atlantic area, and five from the South Central states. These regions correspond to the regional divisions of the Modern Language Association of America. Letters were sent to departments, with subsequent telephone calls when necessary. These follow-up calls were repeated until we received either the reading-list or an explanation of why one was not forthcoming.

Graduate reading-lists at doctorate level were selected whenever possible. The rationale for this choice was that a reading-list for doctorate programmes represents the broadest possible inventory of required works. Combined MA-doctorate lists were used when these were available. Where an institution had independent MA and doctorate reading-lists, the two lists were merged, and duplicate entries were counted only once for that school. Reading-lists at MA level were used when no other option was offered. The fifty-eight lists that comprise this study include twelve doctorate lists or equivalent, six combined lists, ten merged MA-doctorate lists, and thirty MA lists.

A database of these reading-lists was developed and compiled on a University of Delaware mainframe computer, with the assistance of Dr Lawrence Hotchkiss, Lead Consultant/Analyst of the Computing and Network Services Department at the University of Delaware. For each institution we entered the information on the reading-list. Listings included the author and title of each work, and we provided the date of publication and the gender of each author. Erroneous titles were identified and corrected, and listings of the same work under different titles were conflated to produce a single entry, identified by its date of first publication.

We undertook an analysis of the contemporary literature element within this database. 'Contemporary' literature of Spain and Spanish America was defined as consisting of works published in Spanish between 1936 and the present. We selected the starting date because it marks the onset of the Spanish Civil War, and does not conflict with historical markers for Spanish America, where the 'contemporary' period is generally held to begin in 1940. The first questions that we sought to answer were: Which books and authors were represented? and How often did they appear on the lists? To arrive at an answer, we examined the lists to see how many titles, and how many authors (allowing a combination of works) were present on every list. We followed up by determining the proportional representation of every book and author cited, covering all the reading-lists. Percentages were calculated to four decimal places, but expressed to the nearest whole number . We also looked at the distribution of writers and works by gender, to identify women authors. Here we sought to answer the question that is fundamental to contemporary feminist enquiry: How many women writers, and how many works by women writers, are part of the twentieth-century novel canon?

For this paper, we carried our enquiry one step further: How 'deep' is the representation of women writers on graduate reading-lists in the United States? To answer this question, we separated the contemporary novel element on each reading-list into works by men and works by women, and calculated the percentages of novels written by men and novels written by women that are required reading in each institution in both peninsular and Spanish-American literature.

*   *   *   *   *

EACH OF THE SEVENTY-FOUR Spanish faculties that we contacted by mail and telephone provided a reply. Sixteen of them, however, could not be included in this study. Ten did not offer doctorates. Three did not use reading-lists. And three used individually-fashioned rather than faculty-generated lists. The total number of all entries for the reading-lists ranged widely. The shortest list (at the MA level) contained 32 items covering every literary genre, and the longest (a doctorate list) had 995. For the novel, the longest peninsular list featured 137 titles, and the shortest seven. The longest Spanish-American list contained eight-one novels, and the shortest list featuring Spanish-American literature (one institution had none) included five. For peninsular Spanish literature of the contemporary era (1936 to the present), the number of novels on the reading-lists ranged from just two novels to fifty-four. The average number of novel entries was ten (Standard Deviation SD = 8.8), and the median was seven. For the same period in Spanish-American literature, the number of novels for the fifty-seven institutions that had a Spanish-American reading-list ranged from four to fifty-two. The mean number of novels was eighteen (SD = 12.3), and the median fourteen.

For Spain a total of 103 contemporary novels was represented, written by forty-six authors (thirteen of them female). Some authors were cited on many lists; at the other extreme, books were cited only once. Thirteen titles were unspecified: in seventeen instances, students could choose any work by a given author, including Carmen Martín Gaite, Ana María Matute and Mercè Rodoreda, each of whom appeared on two lists. For Spanish America 141 different contemporary titles were represented, written by seventy-one authors (nineteen of them female). As with the peninsular Spanish canon, required reading for Spanish-American fiction included many idiosyncratic selections. Ninety-four works appeared on only one of the lists; free choice was also apparent in the citations of unspecified works, including those by María Luisa Bombal and Rosario Castellanos (each on two lists) and Marta Lynch (who appeared on one).

The question of canonicity depends entirely on a judgement of how widely represented a title or an author must be in order to qualify for admission to the canon. No work or author was represented on 100 per cent of the reading-lists. If 'canonicity' is defined as presence on 75 per cent of the reading-lists, then the list of canonical works short. For Spain there was only one canonical novel: Luis Martín-Santos's 1962 *Tiempo de silencio* was represented on 79 per cent of the lists. The roll-call of canonical authors present on 75 per cent of the lists, determined by counting citations of any one of the author's works on a reading-list, was similar but not identical to the listing of canonical novels. Leading the Spanish author canon was Camilo José Cela, cited on 98 per cent of the lists and followed by Luis Martín-Santos on 79 per cent (an identical percentage to *Tiempo de silencio*). These findings and those immediately following are contained in Figures I and II (below, 55 – 56).

If representation is more generously defined as inclusion on 50 per cent or more of the reading-lists, the canon in twentieth-century literature is expanded. By this measure there were five canonical Spanish novels, none of them written by women, and three more canonical authors, all male. When a canonical work is defined by its presence on only 25 per cent or more of the lists, stretching the definition of 'canonical' to its furthest limits, the listing was broadened considerably. At last, and only in Spain, women writers and their works are included, along with four more texts written by men and two more male authors. The women and the works are identical: Carmen Laforet and *Nada* on 47 per cent of the reading-lists, Carmen Martín Gaite on 41 per cent and *El cuarto de atrás* on 34 per cent, and Ana María Matute on 41 per cent with *Primera memoria* on 33 per cent. No additional women or texts written by women approach Laforet, Matute, and Martín Gaite. The next closest novel, also by Matute, was *Fiesta al noroeste*, and it appeared on only 5 per cent of the total (three, that is, of fifty-eight reading-lists). No other female Spanish author achieved even 5 per cent representation.

As noted at the outset, this goal of this study was to describe the canon for both Spain and Spanish America. However, our findings do not embrace Spanish-American literature by women in a report on the canon. This is because, in the United States of the early 1990s, we found no women writers or texts written by women in the contemporary Spanish-American novel canon. For Spanish America the highest representation achieved is presence on one-fifth of the reading-lists. The two women authors with highest representation are Elena Poniatowska (born in Mexico) on 22 per cent with *Hasta no verte, Jesús mío* on 21 per cent, and Isabel Allende (Chile) on 21 per cent, with *La casa de los espíritus* on 19 per cent. Their nearest women rivals are María Luisa Bombal (Chile) on 16 per cent, and Elena Garro (Mexico) on 14 per cent. Two further texts written by women attained 5 per cent or more: *Los recuerdos del porvenir* by Elena Garro on 14 per cent (eight of the fifty-eight lists) and *La amortajada* by María Luisa Bombal on 12 per cent (seven lists).

The distribution of novels written by women and required reading on the lists, reported here for the first time, is revealing. These findings contain good news and bad news. On the negative side, 24 per cent of the contemporary peninsular Spanish reading-lists (14 of 58 lists) do not contain a single work by a woman author. The positive side of the same data is that 76 per cent (44 of 58 lists) have at least one woman on their list, representing anywhere from 6 to 75 per cent of their total for this period. For Spanish America, the bad news outweighs the good. Over half of the institutions' lists did not contain a single contemporary work by a woman (31 of 57). However, twenty-six institutions (22 per cent) do have one or more texts written by women on their list of required reading, representing from 2 to 38 per cent of the total required reading for this period.

*   *   *   *   *

A CENTRAL FINDING of our study is that there is currently no canon of Spanish or Spanish-American twentieth-century prose fiction, if 'canonical' is defined as a work's presence on every reading-list. Not one novel was selected unanimously by the Spanish faculties we surveyed. Only two authors, one in Spain and one in Hispanic America, achieve canonical status when citation of any work is counted. They are Camilo José Cela, represented on 98 per cent (57 of 58) of the reading-lists, and Gabriel García Márquez, also on 99 per cent (56 of 57) of the lists. It may be that the true canon of contemporary Hispanic prose fiction is restricted to winners of the Nobel Prize for Literature.

If the concept of canonicity is stretched to include representation on half of the lists studied, then a canon emerges. For Spain it comprises five novels, and for Spanish America eight. Each of these novels was published before 1970: two in the 1960s, two in the 1950s, and one in the 1940s from Spain; four in the 1960s, three in the 1950s, and one in the 1940s from Spanish America. By this measure, there are just four canonical authors for Spain and ten for Hispanic America. All of the works are written by men, and all the 'canonical' authors are men.

Only when the definition of the canon is broadened to include representation on one-quarter of the lists analysed do women authors and their texts appear, and then only from Spain. According to this exceedingly generous standard, three peninsular women writers are included: Carmen Laforet (born 1921), Ana María Matute (born 1926), and Carmen Martín Gaite (born 1925).

The exiguous presence of women writers in the contemporary peninsular novel canon – and the absence of Spanish-American women writers – arguably has to do with the process of canon formation. Now a subject of scholarly enquiry in its own right, this process nevertheless remains a bone of contention. Idealists such as Albert Cook believe, as he states in his revealingly titled *Canons and Wisdoms*, that the canon inevitably recognizes 'profound wisdom' (Cook 1993: xi). A more cynical view, expressed by John Guillory in his also aptly titled *Cultural Capital: The Problem of Literary Canon Formation* (1991: 4), is that canon formation seeks to achieve 'explicit political ends'. Realists such as Wendell Harris, who defined the term 'canonicity' in a *PMLA* article with that title, acknowledge that university teachers are inclined to take the path of least resistance, teaching 'what they have been taught, what is easily available in print, what others ... and they themselves are writing about' (Harris 1991: 114).

Regardless of which theory is correct, it is clear that 'standards of literary merit are not absolute but contingent' (Lauter 1991: 107). Certain value judgments are implicit in the reading-list selections of leading institutions of higher learning in the United States. Highest value is assigned to works that have been in print for at least three decades and are written by men. To see whether or not these values are unique to the contemporary era, and whether or not they are enduring, we will need to examine the reading-list data from other eras and genres. That study is under way. We also will need to review graduate reading-lists from the same institutions over time, to see if and how revision takes place as years go by. To understand the admission to the canon of works written by women, it will be instructive to look closely at the three novels that have made it, to see what if any characteristics they share.

*   *   *   *   *

NOW THAT THE PERCENTAGE of women in the canon has been determined, we will focus on the three works that have been admitted to our female canon for the contemporary peninsular novel. These are *Nada* (47 per cent of the US graduate reading-lists), *El cuarto de atrás* (34 per cent) and *Primera memoria* (33 per cent). Specifically, we would like to pose this question: What is it about these works that enabled them to be admitted to what is clearly a male-dominated canon?

Our hypothesis is that three special factors underlie the success of *Nada*, *Primera memoria*, and *El cuarto de atrás*. These are not the factors that first come to mind. The fact that they won prizes (two won the Premio Nadal and the third the Premio Nacional de Literatura), that they have 'aged' enough to ascend to the canon, and that they are extremely well written are prerequisites. (That all three were published by Editorial Destino may be a coincidence.) Other novels that fulfil these criteria – prizes, date of publication, and excellence – are nevertheless excluded, including one by Martín Gaite (*Entre visillos*, 1958) which was on only one of fifty-eight lists.

Examining *Nada, Primera memoria*, and *El cuarto de atrás*, we find three distinguishing characteristics that set them apart from other novels written by women. First, they are accessible to male readers. Second, they are historically significant. And third, they invite multiple critical interpretation.

Accessibility means that men who read *Nada, Primera memoria*, and *El cuarto de atrás* can read *as men*. What do we mean by this? Each of these novels has a male protagonist in addition to a female narrator. The men arrive on the scene early in the novel – Román in *Nada* is introduced after seventeen pages, Borja is present on the very first page of *Primera memoria*, and the man dressed in black in *El cuarto de atrás* enters after the first eighteen pages – and they stay the course of the novel. A male reader who reads these texts is not forced to be a 'resisting reader' – Judith Fetterley's term for women who must enter male worlds, forced to identify with the opposite sex in order to experience a work of literature. Although the main character may describe herself using the feminine gender, she also tells the story of a fascinating male counterpart.

'Historical significance' means that each of these novels is what José Luis Cano called a 'documento de su tiempo'. This characteristic runs counter to the truism that women's novels deal exclusively with the domestic sphere. Even when this environment is highlighted, as in *Nada*, it is clearly a microcosm of the larger world that surrounds it. Not only do all three novels engage with the surrounding society, they each make a brave statement in their own historical contexts. Here we refer to the era of what Juan Goytisolo called 'literatura elusiva-alusiva' for the first two, and the well-known 'plague' of memoirs following Franco's demise for the third. In *Nada*, Laforet demonstrates the decline of the proud bourgeoisie and the lingering conflicts in postwar Barcelona. In *Primera memoria*, Matute gives a miniature portrait of two 'siblings' (actually cousins) whose fathers are fighting on opposite sides in the Spanish Civil War. And, in *El cuarto de atrás*, Martín Gaite evokes the experience of an entire generation in the 'primera posguerra' that was kept under wraps for so long. Marion Holt has published convincing evidence that historical significance is a major factor in determining the contemporary peninsular theatre canon, and we submit that it is a powerful determinant for the novel as well.

Factor number three – attractiveness to us, the critics – is the third common element to these works. We have two measures of critical interest: the quantity and the quality of publications about them. The first is easier to measure. For example, a tabulation of articles devoted to female peninsular writers, published around the same time that the reading-lists were collected in the early 1990s and based on *MLA* bibliographies for the preceding decade, indicates that Laforet, Matute, and Martín Gaite are the three most studied contemporary women writers (Brown 1991: 19).

Quality is more problematic, but at the very least we can document the great variety of critical responses that these novels have elicited. A key characteristic of each of these works is that they invite multiple interpretations. With *Nada*, for example, critics have pointed out many thematic possibilities and debated whether or not its structure is brilliantly effective or is ill-conceived. Since its appearance, the novelistic world of *Primera memoria* has been analysed from many different vantage points, including the semiotic and the religious; and *El cuarto de atrás* has elicited a plethora of critical responses, each highlighting a different aspect of the work. Another subjective but valid measure of high quality criticism is the instantaneous recall by any scholar in the field of key pieces of criticism that shaped or reshaped his or her thinking about a work. Examples include essays by David William Foster and Gustavo Pérez Firmat on *Nada*; writings by Janet Díaz Pérez and Margaret Jones on *Primera memoria*; and analyses by Mirella Servodidio and Linda Gould Levine of *El cuarto de atrás*. The point is that the criticism elicited by these novels is rich, diverse, and ongoing. No one can or has 'said it all' about the texts in our canon written by women which have clearly captured the interest of male as well as female critical readers.

*   *   *   *   *

IN CONCLUSION, we reviewed the contemporary novel canon through statistical analysis of nearly sixty reading-lists from leading doctorate-granting Spanish faculties in the United States. We found that very little agreement exists about the canon, and that the number of works by women on the lists is small. The distribution of women writers on the lists, reported here for the first time, indicates that 76 per cent of peninsular reading-lists (but only 22 per cent of Spanish-American lists) contain at least one work by a woman writer. We can identify three novels, and three authors, that form part the contemporary novel canon: *Nada* (1944) by Carmen Laforet, *Primera memoria* (1960) by

Ana María Matute, and *El cuarto de atrás* (1978) by Carmen Martín Gaite. An analysis of the unique features that these works share – central male characters, historical significance, and critical appeal – may provide clues as to just what it takes for a novel written by a woman to become a classic in the field.

JOAN L. BROWN & CRISTA JOHNSON

University of Delaware

FIGURE I

Representation of Peninsular Novels
on the Reading-Lists, 1936 – Present *

Title	Author	Date	Count (of 58)	Per cent
Tiempo de silencio	L. Martín-Santos	1962	46	79
La familia de Pascual Duarte	C. J. Cela	1942	41	71
La colmena	C. J. Cela	1951	40	69
El Jarama	R. Sánchez Ferlosio	1956	29	50
Señas de identidad	J. Goytisolo	1966	29	50
Nada	C. Laforet	1944	27	47
Reivindicación del conde don Julián	J. Goytisolo	1970	24	41
Cinco horas con Mario	M. Delibes	1966	23	40
El cuarto de atrás	C. Martín Gaite	1978	20	34
Volverás a Región	J. Benet	1967	20	34
Primera memoria	A. M. Matute	1960	19	33
Mosén Millán Réquiem por un campesino español	R. Sender	1953	17	29

* Adapted from Brown & Johnson (1995: 259).

FIGURE II

Representation of Contemporary Peninsular Authors
on the Reading-Lists **

Author	Date of Birth	Gender	Count of (58)	Percent
Camilo José Cela	1916	M	57	98
Luis Martín-Santos	1924	M	46	79
Juan Goytisolo	1931	M	42	72
Rafael Sánchez Ferlosio	1927	M	30	52
Miguel Delibes	1920	M	29	50
Carmen Laforet	1921	F	27	47
Carmen Martín Gaite	1925	F	24	41
Ana María Matute	1926	F	24	41
Juan Benet	1927	M	22	38
Ramón Sender	1902	M	22	38

** Adapted from Brown & Johnson (1995: 259).

ONCE UPON A TIME:
POST-WAR WOMEN WRITERS
AND THE FAIRY-TALE

AMONG THE NUMEROUS STUDIES of the fairy-tale undertaken this century, a growing percentage has begun to examine the genre from feminist perspectives. General accord exists that folk or fairy-tales, often deriving from myth, evolved for untold generations in the oral tradition until written down form the late seventeenth century onwards:

> Almost all critics who have studied the emergence of the literary fairy-tale in Europe agree that educated writers purposely appropriated the oral folk-tale and converted it into a type of literary discourse about mores, values, and manners so that children would become civilized according to the social code of that time.

(Zipes 1988: 3)

Those codes, as feminist writers would see them, were patriarchal, phallocentric, and misogynist. Bruno Bettelheim's 1985 study *The Uses of Enchantment* emphasizes didactic and civilizing functions, interpreting the meaning and importance of fairy-tales from a generally Freudian stance which stresses the Oedipal family and the stories' therapeutic potential in resolving problems of individual development. But neither Bettelheim nor Propp's often cited formalist analysis, *Morphology of the Folk-Tale*, provides much insight into gender relations or other aspects of interest to feminist critics.

Zipes observes that 'studies have shown that the folk-tale originated as far back as the Megalithic period' (1984: 5), and other evidence suggests that certain fairy-tale themes are more ancient still, going back as far as 25 000 BC.[1] Thus, many traits may derive from early tribal or matriarchal cultures, but 'the

---

1. See Marie-Louise von Franz (1970), quoted by Ichiishi (1994: 37), who observes that 'basic motifs have not changed much' despite time and oral transmission.

matriarchal world view and motifs of the original folk-tales underwent successive stages of "patriarchalization"... Matriarchal mythology... had been
transformed [by the Middle Ages]' (Zipes 1988: 7). Consciously crafted forms
of the literary fairy-tale proliferated following an important shift in European
attitudes to sexuality during the sixteenth and seventeenth centuries, as
'restriction and revulsion toward frank sexual behavior replaced open acceptance... the roles of males and females became more rigidly defined' (33).
Fairy-tales with their universal symbols provided ways of dealing with gender
roles, sexuality, initiation, and other 'unspeakable' topics. These tales with
their simplicity become for Jung the simplest expression of the collective psyche, archetypes of the individuation process.

Fairy-tales, constituting universal, age-old allegories, often with connotations of magical or religious nature, do not necessarily contain fairies, although elements of fantasy, the marvellous, or the supernatural are usually
present. Themes are few and remarkably similar, with nearly identical basic
plots, incidents, and characters. The archetypal fairy-tale features a happy
ending which, in some seventy per cent of traditional tales, involves matrimony. Rare exceptions to the happy ending exist – for example, Hans Christian Andersen's *The Little Mermaid* – but the unhappy ending does not alter
basic gender patterns. Sex roles in fairy-tales generally require the heroine's
loss of self: she is 'systematically deprived of affection, stimulation, pleasurable activity, instruction, and even companionship... a totally powerless prisoner' (Waelti-Walters 1982: 1). *Cinderella, Sleeping Beauty, Snow White,
Beauty and the Beast*, and similar tales constitute pro-marriage propaganda,
purveying the message that a woman's appearance should be her sole concern: 'Ugliness in the fairy-tale is generally accepted to be the outward and
manifest sign of wickedness' (45). Valued only for her beauty, the heroine fits
the situation of women described by Simone de Beauvoir: 'Long before the
eventual mutilation [of ageing], woman is haunted by the horror of growing
old... It is necessary for her to be attractive, to please; she is allowed no hold
on the world save through the mediation of some man' (1964: 575 – 76). The
female's only security consists in being loved by the father or his substitute.
Little wonder that recent women writers have increasingly turned to subverting the fairy-tale.

The patriarchal establishment has long used fairy-tales to buttress the
situation de Beauvoir describes, reinforcing atavistic notions of sex roles and

the traditional ideology of male domination. Some such tales have been seen as racist as well as sexist, representing white-European cultural values while upholding male privilege; most present money and property as prime goals, while magic and miracles provide resolution of social problems (Zipes 1986: 6). Works such as Madonna Kolbenschlag's *Kiss Sleeping Beauty Goodbye* (1979) and Colette Dowling's *The Cinderella Complex* (1981) contend that fairy-tales promote feminine psychological dependency and are thus responsible for women allowing themselves to be oppressed. Numerous feminist critics 'feel that the fairy-tales of their childhood stamp their present actions and behaviour' (Zipes 1986: 9).

Several contemporary Spanish women novelists depict formative influences of childhood readings upon the adult female psyche, without distinguishing between traditional fairy-tales and modern books for children such as J. M. Barrie's *Peter Pan* or Lewis Carroll's *Alice's Adventures in Wonderland and Through the Looking-Glass.*[2] Evoking the overall context of female socialization in a phallocentric culture, Spanish women writers especially indict convent schooling and reactionary socio-religious influences. Curiously, 'the attitude toward women in Christianity and in fairy-tales is remarkably similar. The choice in each case lies between a Mary and a Mary Magdalene, sanctified virginity or vilified sex, princess/dead mother or stepmother/witch' (Waelti-Walters 1982: 80) – a dichotomy buttressed by *machista* culture in post-Civil-War Spain where the focus of female socialization was upon matrimony. Most fairy-tale models reinforce male hegemony, and the motifs of marriage and happiness-ever-after are among the elements most frequently subverted by contemporary women writers.

Although Spain has not produced specialists in the feminist fairy-tale *per se* (in the tradition of writers such as Angela Carter, Tanith Lee, Meghan Collins, and Ursula LeGuin), post-war women writers including Ana María Matute, Carmen Martín Gaite, Teresa Barbero, Esther Tusquets, and Nuria Pompeia do refer specifically to fairy-tales.[3] Matute and Martín Gaite have written original fairy-tales with feminist undertones. The feminist fairy-tale

---

2.   As there are traditional fairy-tales without fairies, as well as modern exemplary or didactic tales for children by writers such as Hans Christian Andersen which have neither magic nor fantasy yet are termed fairy-tales, and because *Peter Pan* and *Alice in Wonderland* do involve fantasy and magic, this study includes them in the general category of fairy-tales.

3.   Pompeia, primarily a cartoonist, hilariously lampoons Spain's brainwashing of its future women in *Maternasis* (1967), *Y fueron felices comiendo perdices* (1970), and *Mujercitas* (1975).

usually promotes 'feminist demands for gender rearrangement and equality in the family and at the work place' (Zipes 1988: 32) – demands more clearly enunciated by Tusquets and by writers who are younger than those of the Franco era.

Conventional fairy-tales, like the quest romance or initiatory tale, symbolically reflect rites of passage or initiation into the adult community. As the novice undergoes the ritual ordeal, he or she experiences a basic existential change, emerging as another.[4] Unlike traditional tales which reinforce the *status quo*, feminist fairy-tales (usually written for older readers) take issue with misogynist traditions that humiliate and punish non-conforming women – a point subtly but unmistakably made by Matute in 'La oveja negra', for example. Feminist fairy-tales show women using their wits, attaining independence, and seeking mutual respect (as in the two tales by Martín Gaite). Feminist fairy-tales examine sexual politics and relations of power in society, subvert the notion of marriage as necessity or goal, and expose the dangers to women of self-denial and self-betrayal. Some Spanish women novelists adapt the *Bildungsroman* to these ends (Matute's *Primera memoria* is a case in point), incorporating fairy-tale motifs and references, subverting traditional endings, or emphasizing unconventional attitudes. Their use of fairy-tale materials deliberately exposes the truth/reality interface and the negative consequences for feminine socialization of internalizing fairy-tale social codes.

Utilization of fairy-tale motifs varies from minimal intertextual allusions or citations (Barbero) to complex intertextual mosaics (Tusquets), and even wholesale incorporation of structures, situations, and characters (Martín Gaite). Minimal fairy-tale intertextuality acquires special significance when given symbolic overtones, as in Teresa Barbero's *El último verano en el espejo* (1967). This novel begins with an epigraph from *Alice in Wonderland*: '¡Oh! –pensó Alicia–. ¡Qué mundo tan maravilloso debe haber al otro lado del espejo!' The concepts of wonderland, ideal happiness, and escaping from unpleasant reality 'through the looking-glass' surface at turning points in the protagonist's life, and the mirror becomes a multivalent symbol. Marta, the protagonist, recalls her mother's huge, decorative mirror, 'lo mismo que en el

---

4.   Mircea Eliade's analysis (1958) identifies seven fundamental patterns: separation from the mother, symbolic death and rebirth, going into the wilderness (dark forest, etc.), fights with magical or animal aid, descent into the underworld, ordeals and impossible tasks, and epiphany or discovery of hidden truths. Most of these are easily identifiable in *The Snow Queen*, for example, and in Martín Gaite's novelistic adaptation of it, *La reina de las nieves*.

cuento de Alicia' (73), representing childhood dreams of a marvellous world on the other side: 'Esto solía ocurrirme cuando la vida en mi hogar me resultaba excesivamente triste y monótona' (73).[5] In moments of depression and disillusion, Marta yearns for life beyond the mirror: 'Seguramente allí está la felicidad' (127).

The happily-ever-after motif also characterizes the *novela rosa*, the paperback romance read by the adolescent Marta and her friend Elena: ' – "Y fueron felices, felices, eternamente..." Elena cerró de golpe la novela. – Todas acaban lo mismo y una se siente muy tranquila de que sea así' (127). Like fairy-tales, the *novela rosa* purveyed the phallocentric myth of matrimony as paradise, brainwashing young women whose rudimentary education prepared them only for domesticity, closing the door to careers, autonomy, and self-realization.   Emblematic of generations of young women raised on dreams of marital bliss, Marta at thirty finds herself trapped in a frustrating marriage, lacking the courage to leave an alcoholic husband and accompany her lover to America.   Condemned to the endless repetition of menial domestic tasks, possibly pregnant, existentially alone, Marta wanders sleeplessly through her darkened home, wondering aloud, 'realmente, ¿estuve alguna vez al otro lado del espejo?' (265).   Barbero's strategic intertextual use of the looking-glass and Wonderland motifs juxtaposes and contrasts dreams and reality, myths and daily life, past innocence and present disillusionment.   Her minimal fairy-tale intertextuality symbolically indicts traditional education, subverting myths used to foment passive feminine acceptance of traditional gender roles, patriarchal values, and masculine domination.

Ana María Matute's fairy-tales for younger readers are more conventional and add nothing to a study of her use of the genre for feminist ends.   Fairy-tale references in *Primera memoria* (1960) begin with Matia's memories of: 'Kay y Gerda, en su jardín sobre el tejado', 'La Joven Sirena abrazada a la estatua', 'Los Once Príncipes Cisnes' (16).[6]   Kay and Gerda (from *The Snow*

---

5.   Mirrors function not only as escape motifs, but vehicles of existential self-encounter in the present. They facilitate contact with the past, allowing Marta to resuscitate her adolescent self by gazing fixedly within: 'Allí estaba "Alicia": una "Alicia" de catorce años, mirándose al espejo... queriendo evadirse, cruzar al otro lado, encontrarse a sí misma' (Barbero 1967: 126).

6.   Matute also alludes to various 'little people', including 'el viejo Trasgo de Doure, coronado de carámbanos y piñas, cuando la Séptima Princesita del Cerro de los Duendes le tomó por la muñeca' (1960: 191). Elves and other fantasy figures combine with Es Mariné's tales of adventure, diabolic spells, and pirate treasure to evoke the childhood mentality (but without the symbolism of loss attached to Kay and Gerda, the Little Mermaid, and Peter Pan). See also

Queen) and the Little Mermaid represent the lost paradise of childhood. Matute's fairy-tales sometimes replace traditional characterization, as when Matia situates herself inside her readings, ironically gazing into the steamy bathroom mirror:

> 'Alicia en el mundo del espejo,' pensé, más de una vez, contemplándome en él, desnuda y desolada, con un gran deseo de atravesar su superficie... Tristísima imagen aquella – la mía –, de ojos asustados, que era, tal vez, la imagen misma de la soledad.
>
> (73)

Peter Pan and Neverland (115) signify Paradise Lost, Matia's private childhood world, emblematically represented by her black doll, Gorogó. Matia mentally equates battles between the island gangs with those of Peter Pan and the Lost Boys against the pirates and Captain Hook and terms Borja 'desterrado Peter Pan, como yo misma' (162). Her Peter-Pan complex produces a conscious desire not to lose her childhood innocence: 'deseara gritar y decir: "Oh, no, no, detenedme, por favor. Detenedme, yo no sabía hacia dónde corría, no quiero conocer nada más." (Pero ya había saltado el muro y dejado atrás a Kay y Gerda, en su jardín sobre el tejado.)' (163). Leaving Kay and Gerda behind signifies Matia's loss of the garden of innocence, her discovery of a 'real' world of conflict, alcohol, sexuality, perversion, and violence.[7]

After Borja's betrayal of Manuel and her own mute complicity, however, and before her own imminent departure, Matia faces the definitive loss of childhood with these thoughts: '(No existió la Isla de Nunca Jamás y la Joven Sirena no consiguió un alma inmortal, porque los hombres y las mujeres no aman, y se quedó con un par de inútiles piernas, y se convirtió en espuma.) Eran horribles los cuentos' (243). The Little Mermaid represents desire, the need to be loved: 'La Joven Sirena quería que la amasen, pero nunca la amó nadie. ¡Pobre sirena! ¿Para eso se tuvo que parecer a los humanos?' (82–83). The adult narrator retrospectively identifies with the mermaid: 'Acaso, sólo deseaba que alguien me amara alguna vez' (83). Matute's inter-

---

Stephen Hart's discussion of fairy-tale intertextuality in *Primera memoria*, Tusquets's *El mismo mar de todos los veranos*, and Martín Gaite's *El cuarto de atrás* (1993: 63–87).

7.   Matute's use of Kay and Gerda as symbols of an ideal lost childhood world differs considerably from Martín Gaite's adaptation of the quest romance format and rites of passage topos. The Peter-Pan motif is used differently by Tusquets, for whom the 'flight from maturity' emerges as much more negative than for Matute.

textual tapestry evokes the mentality of her protagonist-narrator, representing the conflict of ideal and real, of dream and waking, magic and the everyday world.

In the three tales of *Tres y un sueño* (1961), Matute adopts the fairy-tale mode to evoke the dream of childhood (an Edenic state preceding adult awareness), to symbolize rites of passage and portray three possible outcomes to leaving the garden of innocence. In 'La razón', faithfully imitating Hans Christian Andersen, Ivo, a neglected, exploited orphan and solitary dreamer, may be the last person left on earth for whom fantasy is real. Gnomes and elves (who need people to believe in them to continue existing) take Ivo to live in a magic underground world for many years so that he will not forget them. But when he finally returns, grown up and having acquired 'reason', he seeks work, and the little people are turned to ashes. In 'La Isla', lonely, rich, eight-year-old Perico plays hookey, visiting a fair where urchins steal his clothes and shoes; he trades his remaining possessions for a chance to shoot at winning a prize island. Suddenly alone and freezing at the seaside, his vision of the golden island coincides with his death.

As in *Los niños tontos*, some children die and others grow up, but a few with the Peter-Pan syndrome grow physically without ceasing mentally to be children. This third possibility appears in Matute's allegorical autobiography, 'La oveja negra', whose nameless protagonist, 'ella', is deemed bad because, unlike fairy-tale girls, she is not pretty, nor obedient, nor good. After she creates the black doll, Tomboctú (emblematic of childhood and comparable to Gorogó in *Primera memoria*), the dog Lucio destroys him and she sets out into the world seeking the lost talisman. Notable among subsequent disconnected, nightmarish events are the symbolic murder of her grandmother, encounters with black boys whom she identifies as Cain and Abel, and meeting the operator of a puppet theatre, 'el gran farsante', 'embustero' (Matute 1961: 85). He feeds her, locks her in his trailer, and later smashes the puppets, demanding her aid in pulling the wagon out of the mire, taking her jewellery, and denouncing her selfishness.[8] Later, her captor demands her repentance but she denies having sinned (90–91). Some shanty-town women feed and shelter the protagonist, but expect her to conform to gender roles: 'Debes decir siempre que sí. Tú, calla y asiente. Anda, ayúdanos a recoger los platos' (95). When

---

8.   Matute portrays her marriage as financial exploitation by a spoilt ne'er-do-well, making it tempting to read this text as an allegory of her marriage.

she attempts to board a train with the men, the women hold her back. Amid scenes of war and holocaust, these women develop relationships with the invaders, sewing and mending for them, and showing them affection: 'Las mujeres la reprendían a menudo, porque ella no hacía ninguna de estas cosas' (99).[9] After prolonged wandering, stoned and bleeding, she is saved by an organ-grinder and carried to a vacant lot, from where her brothers – now adult businessmen – take her to her grandmother's deserted mountain home. Amid ruins, she plays with the area children, still insisting she is a child.

Essentials of the quest romance include the wandering or pilgrimage, growth, and return to the point of origin. Certain episodes appear fantastic because the narrator's remains uncomprehending. Surreal, oneiric qualities and abrupt shifts, combined with unexplained or arbitrary actions and reactions, contribute to the reader's experience of the tale as uncanny. Matute appropriates the fairy-tale format, without fairies, to exorcise personal demons, conveying her rejection of patriarchal values and traditional models of matrimony and motherhood. Her protest against customary gender roles and the exclusion of women from the 'men's world' of literature extends to other women's connivance in preventing her escape from the *encierro* imposed by society.

Esther Tusquets, in *El mismo mar de todos los veranos* (1978) employs an extensive intertextual network of fairy-tale allusions, combined with myths, in particular the myth of Ariadne, Theseus, and the Minotaur. Various critics have noted similarities between fairy-tales and classical myths, pointing to common themes and motifs, the presence of giants and monsters, enchanters, sirens, and similar figures in both genres. *El mismo mar* has been examined by several myth critics, but much less attention has been paid to the fairy-tale elements. Ichiishi observes that among several techniques with which Tusquets challenges the 'absolute authority of the phallocentric discourses which have governed her characters' existence' is her 'strategic and complex use of fairy-tale motifs' (1994: 36–37). Despite suggesting the basis for a feminist examination of Tusquets's use of fairy-tales, Ichiishi adopts a Jungian perspective, viewing *The Little Mermaid* as 'a failed quest for individuation or psychic unity' (37) within the context of a narrative of female development.

---

9.   Writing under the Franco censorship, Matute employed allegory and understatement to subvert the misogynist attitudes and acculturation which made these women accomplices in their own exploitation and that of other women.

For this critic, 'the fairy-tale elements... dispersed throughout the narrative are sedimentations of childhood fantasies which have survived into adulthood' (61). Tusquets's protagonist usually identifies with 'archetypal symbols of the feminine. She especially relates to innocent female characters who suffer for love: Rapunzel, Sleeping Beauty, the Little Mermaid, Beauty [of *Beauty and the Beast*], Ariadne, Isolde, Brünhilde' (67).

The nameless protagonist of *El mismo mar* reconstructs her past life, emphasizing her childhood and her university years some three decades before, utilizing an extensive fairy-tale intertext which refers primarily to childhood. A few motifs subversively recall other time planes, and facilitate characterization, irony, burlesque, and critique. The prince, emblematic of male hegemony and the myth of matrimony as paradise, emerges as the fairy-tale motif most consistently subverted, not simply charming but 'el más bello y más tonto de los príncipes'. Tusquets pairs countervailing adjectives to subversive effect: 'el Príncipe Encantador – siempre un poquito bobo aunque no sea esta vez el más tonto, ni tampoco el más bello de los príncipes' (1978: 32). The protagonist's internal monologue during her first meeting with Clara demythologizes Andersen's prince who was not even under a spell: 'fue simplemente un poco bobo, y en sus ojos distantes nunca hubo misterio, fue sólo bobería, incomprensión radical...' (66–67).[10] Further subverting the myth of romantic love, she reflects that, for the Little Mermaid, the worst is not the prince's marrying 'la más vulgar y anodina y cotidiana de las princesas' nor even knowing she will never win a human soul. 'Lo peor y más triste es descubrir que el príncipe encantador es también... el más vulgar de los príncipes' (170). Consistent demythologization of the idealized bridegroom subverts the masculine archetype, romantic love, and fairy-tale marriage.[11]

---

10. The scene at the opera presents Clara as uninterested in 'muchachas inocentonas abandonadas en su noche de bodas por príncipes perversos o inconstantes, esas muchachas que viven con repetido fervor una historia de amor que terminará irremisiblemente mal' (133). Demythologizing fairy-tale romance during unrestrained lovemaking with Clara in the darkened theatre, the narrator forgets the stage: 'y las princesas cisne, las muchachas abandonadas en la noche de bodas, las sirenas enamoradas, aletean, se estremecen, agonizan en los brazos de un príncipe de cartón, y quedan lejos' (138). Tusquets implicitly equates phallocentric Francoist mythology with the unreality of fairy-tale operas, ironically ridiculing both.

11. Demythologization of conjugal bliss continues when the narrator allows Julio to pressure her into returning, and to take her to bed in a place termed 'una caja para mariposas muertas, una caja de coleccionista a dimensiones siderales... el hombre coleccionista me manipula, me dispone' (Tusquets 1978: 214). Later, the metaphor is sustained by characterizing the husband's brutal love-making as 'pinning' her with his phallus.

Tusquets's most important fairy-tale intertexts concern Clara or the narrator. Treated as an intruder in a library (still a masculine domain), the protagonist reflects ironically that 'hasta los atildados gatos de Cheshire que han
perdido en el aire la sonrisa, nos miran mal' (52). The narrator equates Clara
with Peter Pan (60-61); she is termed boyish or childlike in appearance:
'sorprendentemente flaca, sorprendentemente joven' (60); and the novel has
this epigraph: 'Y Wendy creció.' These become Clara's final words of farewell after the narrator has abandoned her (229). Clara is also identified with
the Little Mermaid: 'tiernísima sirena de senos adolescentes y hermosa cola
casi piernas' (66). Upon taking Clara home, the narrator mentally terms the
house 'el fondo ultimísimo de mi mundo subterráneo' (84); later the girl becomes 'una ondina' (136). Fairy-tale identifications multiply: 'Cuál de las dos
es la Bella? Y en qué rincón nos espera la Bestia?' (84). Clara, linked with
Ariadne, an Aztec goddess, Angelica (87), and Rapunzel (93), proteically becomes 'Clara gato, Clara princesa más oriental que nunca' (89). Alluding to
The Princess and the Pea and the test of the authentic princess, Clara's per-
ceptiveness qualifies her as 'mi princesa guisante de piel sensible' (96). Amid
oblique references to *The Emperor and the Nightingale* (103-04), Clara acquires further avian identities, 'cisne negro, mi patito feo enfurruñado' (106).
      Beauty and the Beast and Peter Pan become metaphors for the narrator's
relationship with Clara: 'y ahora sé que las dos somos la Bella y las dos somos
igualmente la Bestia' (183). Peter-Pan motifs multiply, as the narrator recounts her early life with fairy-tale rhetoric (189, 191). Clara's unconditional
love makes her the narrator's shadow, 'la sombra tal vez encontrada de una
mujer que perdió hace mucho su sombra' (197). Later, realizing that she
lacks the strength not to betray Clara, she muses: 'ni ganas tengo... de
emprender juntas la ruta hacia las tierras de Nunca Jamás' (228). For the
narrator, Clara's farewell words, 'Y Wendy creció', signify that Clara had
understood her, but Wendy's growing up meant her leaving Neverland forever
to become a bourgeois housewife, the fate of passive cloistering to which the
narrator returns, unaware of Clara's irony. Tusquets's complex mosaic of
fairy-tale allusions underscores and exposes the unreality of the world
purveyed by Francoist myth, paperback romances, and prescribed fictions for
young women: the world for which they are prepared by the patriarchal
establishment could only exist in Neverland.

Carmen Martín Gaite's repeated references to fairy-tales in *El cuarto de atrás* and *Nubosidad variable* must be left for another occasion. Her most extensive incorporation of the fairy-tale format, however, occurs in *Dos relatos fantásticos* (1986) and *La Reina de las Nieves* (1994). *Dos relatos fantásticos* comprises two tales previously published separately, 'El castillo de las tres murallas' (1983) and 'El pastel del diablo' (1985), both written around the time she began work on *La Reina de las Nieves*.[12] Both atemporal tales feature female protagonists who reject traditional patriarchal values and rebel against oppressive gender roles that marginalize women. In 'El castillo de las tres murallas' tripartite formulas abound: not only does the castle have three walls, but three moats, and three colours (red, black, and green). Lucandro, paranoid owner of the seemingly impenetrable fortress, lacks friends and social relationships, seldom goes out, and never rests or enjoys his domain: 'Siempre pensaba que le estaban engañando y que de ninguno se podía fiar' (Martín Gaite 1986: 13). Separated from the rest of the world not only by walls and moats but also by gardens and mountains, the castle is protected by monster rats called *brundas* in the interior moat, while 'la verja enorme que guardaba la entrada del castillo era toda de hierro sobredorado y tenía en el centro un aldabón grande en forma de dragón' (15). Literally and figuratively, the Gothic isolation and enclosure are complete.

A stairway to the castle symbolizes time with three hundred and sixty-five steps divided into four sections bearing the names of the seasons, and 'cada treinta escalones había rellanos amplios para descansar' (17). Sculpted on the left banister, zodiac signs, hieroglyphics, and ancient historical events signify the past, facing an uncarved right-hand side representing the unknown future. Everywhere, clocks are stopped, for Lucandro hates time's passing: 'estaba rodeado de objetos sin vida que le esclavizaban' (18). Aggravating Lucandro's fear of death is the traumatic thought of others inheriting his possessions. As in the tales of Hans Christian Andersen, sterile materialism is opposed to spiritual and emotional wealth. But Martín Gaite also comments on women's lot, their marginalization and *encierro*, their lack of autonomy. Lucandro lives with Serena, a young beauty who cares nothing for the treasures received as wedding gifts. Lucandro locks them away, leaving her quarters

12. This interest in the fantastic appears in *El cuarto de atrás* (1978) alongside references to Todorov, as well as in the detailed theoretical discussion of the genre in *El cuento de nunca acabar* (1983).

bare: 'y así se parecían más de verdad a la cárcel que eran' (33). Not only is Serena a possession for Lucandro, but the couple probably represent the traditional Spanish marriage. Lucandro symbolizes hereditary status, traditional patriarchal values, and the weight of a static past. As estrangement between the couple grows, Lucandro begins to resemble the *brundas*, a metamorphosis Serena compares to those of fairy-tales (35). Cambof, the ancient resident soothsayer who claims several previous incarnations, recalls being a princess, unable to travel or communicate: 'Nadie hablaba conmigo ni me consultaba nada. Todo lo decidían los demás por mí' (37). According to Costa (1991), the cloistered oblivion of many a fairy-tale princess was the lot of most women under Franco.

When Serena bears a daughter, Altalé, Lucandro's manic possessiveness extends to her: 'Serena se dio cuenta de que él consideraba a la niña como objeto de su exclusiva pertenencia... [que] acabaría por quitársela, como todos los regalos de valor' (40). Like her mother, the girl is a prisoner, with bars on her windows: 'toda la gran habitación parecía una jaula' (42). When the child turns four, Lucandro separates mother and daughter, and Serena languishes until one day Altalé's music teacher sings 'la historia de un prisionero que oía cantar a los pájaros a través de las rejas de la cárcel' (48). While the child concludes that the castle is a prison, Serena and the music teacher elope, vanishing as if by magic. Altalé defies Lucandro's prohibitions, seeking her mother throughout adolescence; meanwhile, her father acquires more rat-like traits and the reputation of a madman. Eventually, Altalé escapes to find her own future with the young rebel, Amir. When she flees, Lucandro disappears and the number of *brundas* increases from twelve to thirteen. 'El castillo de las tres murallas' qualifies as a legitimate feminist fairy-tale, notwithstanding the lack of fairies. Both feminine figures reject patriarchal domination, taking the initiative and acting decisively to seek self-realization. While Serena accepted her object status for several years, her escape from marital tyranny proves the more dramatic, being atypical for the fairy-tale format since she chooses adultery. (Mothers abandon their children in fairy-tales, but not for freedom or for another man.)

In 'El pastel del diablo' another intrepid young heroine, Sorpresa – restless, malcontent, rebellious, and brilliant – learns all that the schoolmaster can offer. He recommends further study but her parents disagree, discussing work options; meanwhile, Sorpresa paints, dreams, and writes stories which she tells to Pizco, an older boy. One summer night, drawn by the sound of revelry, she slips alone through the woods to the Casa Grande, entering unnoticed and exploring unobserved until she finally comes upon the aged owner, forgotten by his guests, drinking alone. After extended conversation, he dons a devil costume, leaving her a piece of amber, and Sorpresa seeks a forest witching place to cast her spell: *grow-grow-grow/know-know-know*. Later, more enthusiastic than ever in telling her stories, she fails to notice that she has lost her interlocutor, for Pizco has become enamoured of an 'older woman'. This initiatory tale, a version of rites of passage, highlights the moment when Sorpresa realizes her creative gift and learns the power of self-sufficiency:

> Alzó los ojos al cielo y se dio cuenta de que estaba completamente sola en el mundo, sin más compañía que aquel motorcito invisible que fabricaba imágenes por dentro de su cabeza... Era una sensación de poder casi diabólico.

> (Martín Gaite 1986: 171)

Ultimately, Martín Gaite's intrepid feminine heroine persuades her parents to let her return to school. 'El pastel del diablo' lacks fantasy elements and derives most of its magic from portraying the child's mind and evoking the magical lure of the unknown.

In *La Reina de las Nieves* Martín Gaite appropriates outright Andersen's tale of *The Snow Queen*, retaining the essentials of plot, characters, and title. Andersen's tale, mirrored on a larger scale in characters and crucial incidents, provides the major structuring device and thus demands brief recapitulation. Two young Nordic neighbours, a boy, Kay, and a girl, Gerda, best friends from infancy, share untrammelled communication as each other's ideal interlocutor. Approximately at the age of puberty, Kay is wounded in the eye by a crystal fragment from a demonic mirror, scorns Gerda for the company of older boys, and vanishes after hitching his sledge to the sleigh of a coldly beautiful mystery woman. Kidnapped by the Snow Queen, Kay remains in her ice palace in the frozen North, blinded to life. Gerda bravely sets forth to find him, and most of the story – unusual for a fairy-tale in its presentation of a heroic (but not necessarily beautiful) female quester – recounts her overcoming multiple trials until, years later, she locates Kay. Gerda's joy turns to sorrow at his indifference, and her copious tears fall upon the malevolent ice splinter and melt it, freeing him from the Snow Queen's power. Upon returning home, both have become adults. Despite the title, the Snow Queen herself is neither heroine nor protagonist. Martín Gaite highlights the miraculous healing power of tears; the fairy-tale motif of bewitching or stealing children; the frozen alienation and solitude of the young male protagonist; his incarceration; and the quest motif, which becomes a dual quest. Separation from childhood home and ties, the loss of significant affective bonds, and the deep-seated need for an idealized interlocutor – for communication *per se* – likewise play major roles.

In *La Reina de las Nieves*, the lighthouse-keeper of an unnamed village on the Atlantic coast raises his orphaned granddaughter, Casilda, who is tutored by the village schoolmaster. She befriends Eugenio, the sickly heir of the neighbouring Villalba estate, La Quinta Blanca. Their relationship mirrors the childhood of Kay and Gerda. When they are older, Casilda rejects Eugenio's offer of marriage, preferring her own self-fulfilment quest. Married through family pressure to a cold, sterile, wealthy beauty, Eugenio demands that Casilda fulfil her secret childhood oath to grant his wish by bearing him a son. This she does. His wife, Gertrudis, remains unaware of the child's parentage, and the couple adopt Leonardo, who never bonds with his putative mother, a pale, frigid, life-denying 'Reina de las Nieves'. Leonardo resides mainly with his grandmother, living in books and fantasy, making Kay and Gerda's world his own. When his grandmother dies, Leonardo plunges deeply into drugs and alcoholism, gratuitous sex, and delinquency during some five years or more, metaphorically freezing his heart. His imprisonment on drug-trafficking charges mirrors Kay's captivity, a contemporary updating of *The Snow Queen*.

Leonardo's release coincides with his parents' death in an car accident: later, Leonardo discovers letters revealing Eugenio's enduring love for another woman, now owner of La Quinta Blanca, his grandmother's manor. More than half the novel is taken up with Leonardo's quest for the pieces to the puzzle – something of a detective investigation aided by fairy-tale coincidences. He learns that the mystery woman is a celebrated essayist and recognizes her style as that of the mystery woman's letters. Even before accepting Casilda's invitation to visit La Quinta Blanca, Leonardo intuits their connection; their extraordinary resemblance confirms that she is his mother and, as in Andersen's tale, their mutual tears melt his frozen heart. Updated to the last quarter of the twentieth century and filled with jet-set motifs, existential absurdity, rampant consumerism, delinquency, and the drug subculture, *La*

Reina de las Nieves repeats *The Snow Queen*'s mythic framework, quest motifs, and initiatory journey. Innumerable intertextual passages, pervasive metafictional references and self-reflective meditations reinforce the structural parallels.[13] The fourth chapter of the tale, entitled 'El rapto de Kay', echoes the quest romance with the solar hero's (Leonardo's) 'fall' or visit to the Inferno (prison), his passage through Purgatory (the lower regions of Madrid's counter-culture), his overcoming darkness (delinquency), and his self-purification and eventual return as an enlightened adult to the point of origin, the rites of passage now complete.

Martín Gaite makes the mirror more significant than it is in Andersen's tale.[14] *La Reina de las Nieves* abounds in references to mirrors and self-conscious literary situations, mirroring or reflecting narratological devices. In the more than three hundred dense pages of her novel, fairy-tale simplicity and abstraction of character are replaced by considerable psychological complexity, and the stylized mythic scenarios become detailed contemporary settings reflecting the post-Franco scene in Spain at the end of the twentieth century. Another major modification consists in Martín Gaite's having made the quest a dual one, giving Kay and Leonardo a collaborative role in their own rehabilitation or redemption, thereby promoting gender equality and hence representing a move beyond more militant feminism.

While Spanish women writers have produced relatively few feminist fairy-tales, they have none the less begun to rewrite the genre from women's perspectives, perhaps not re-establishing a matriarchal world view, but subverting pro-marriage propaganda, presenting autonomous gender models, and otherwise incorporating subtle but profound revisionism.

JANET PÉREZ

Texas Tech University

---

13. See, for example, Martín Gaite (1994: 40, 62, 85, 95, 97–99, 121, 153–55, 175, 201, 225, 250).

14. For an extensive examination of Martín Gaite's use of the mirror, see Pérez (1995).

BEYOND THE FANTASTIC:
NEW TALES FROM FERNÁNDEZ CUBAS

THE WORD MOST OFTEN USED to describe the short stories of Cristina Fernández Cubas is 'fantastic': fantastic, always, in the colloquial sense of 'extraordinarily good'; fantastic, frequently, in the restricted sense of a literary mode.[1] In Tzvetan Todorov's terms, that mode, in which the reader is fully integrated into the world of the protagonist, leaves both of them vacillating between absolute faith and total disbelief as to the 'reality' of bizarre events (Todorov 1970: 35). The resulting 'instability of narrative is at the centre of the fantastic as a mode' (Jackson 1981: 34). When a rational explanation is provided, the work shifts from the fantastic to the uncanny (Freud's *Unheimlich*, Todorov's *étrange*). As Rosemary Jackson suggests (1981: 34), fantastic narratives 'assert that what they are telling is real' but then proceed to introduce what is manifestly unreal: 'They pull the reader from the apparent familiarity and security of the known and everyday world into something more strange, into a world whose improbabilities are closer to the realm normally associated with the marvellous.'

All eight of the tales included in Fernández Cubas's first two collections – *Mi hermana Elba* (1980) and *Los altillos de Brumal* (1983) – fit such descriptions of the fantastic. With the considerable success of these volumes, the name of Cristina Fernández Cubas has become inextricably linked with the fantastic. Although the first scholarly reference to Fernández Cubas's stories of which I am aware (Bellver 1982) fails to classify *Mi hermana Elba* as fantastic literature, almost all subsequent critical studies of her stories do, sometimes with the word directly expressed in the title (Zatlin 1987, Talbot 1989, Ortega 1992), sometimes with such related approaches as the 'recuperation of the semiotic' (Bretz 1988) or 'Gothic indecipherability and doubling' (Glenn 1992).

---

1. This essay partly overlaps with Zatlin (1996).

I would contend, however, that among the four stories contained in the collection *El ángulo del horror* (1990), none truly belongs to the fantastic mode or even to the Gothic genre, despite the fact that scholars have so classified them. Two of these stories are serious in tone and two are humorous; all lend themselves to realistic, psychological interpretations. The crux of the problem – apart from the adherent properties of critical labels – is that, fantastic or not, Fernández Cubas's stories bear her unmistakable stamp. Catherine Bellver, perhaps vacillating to some extent herself, has captured this aspect in her review of the volume:

> The characters and places of each of her four stories are realistic, but a certain quality of the unreal runs through them. Never verging on the fantastic, these stories nonetheless incorporate the elements of the strange and the slightly unusual that characterize Fernández Cubas's fiction.

(Bellver 1991: 372)

In this respect, most of her narratives comply with Jackson's more general definition of literary fantasy, which does not invent unreal worlds but rather (1981: 8) inverts 'elements of this world, recombining its constitutive features in new relations to produce something strange, unfamiliar and *apparently* "new" absolutely "other", and different'.

These, of course, are not the only characteristics that underscore the narrative of Fernández Cubas, whether within or beyond the fantastic mode. Her works typically include some combination of the following: parody, intertextuality, and metafiction, including emphasis on oral story-telling; humour and irony; a fascination with language, the non-verbal, and the failure of communication systems; and identity crises, madness, and other psychoanalytic concerns. As is true of these elements, her repeated use of doubles, mirrors, and enclosures, particularly attics, may or may not be indicators of the fantastic or the Gothic – at least as I shall define them. We might say that her stories tend to explore the mysteries of both external reality and of the human psyche. Most of them, including some that fall outside the fantastic mode, explore inner worlds of fantasy and unconscious desires.

There is a seven-year gap between the appearance of the first collections of her stories and *El ángulo del horror*. During this period Fernández Cubas published her first novel: *El año de Gracia* (1985).[2] Three recent studies ap-

---

2.   A second novel, *El columpio*, appeared in 1995.

proach the novel as postmodernist metafiction or in terms of its intertextual relationships with literary precedents (Bellver 1992, Gleue 1992, and Margenot 1993). On the other hand, Kathleen Glenn (1992) places the novel in the category of Gothic, examining it along with three of the early fantastic tales and two stories from *El ángulo del horror*: 'Helicón' and 'La Flor de España'. That the author might be unhappy with such an epithet is clear from Glenn's interview with her. 'Bueno, muy, muy de acuerdo no estoy,' Fernández Cubas says, conceding that there might be some Gothic elements, 'como también pueden encontrarse elementos fantásticos. Ahora, de eso a meterme en un cajón de literatura gótica, en una etiqueta, no creo, francamente, no creo' (Glenn 1993: 359).

Although I shall focus here on the recent collection of stories, *Con Ágatha en Estambul* (1994), I shall first examine *El ángulo del horror*. Besides Glenn's analysis from the perspective of the Gothic (albeit a loosely defined modern variant), we have José Ortega's commentary, which places both 'El ángulo del horror' and 'Helicón' in the category of the fantastic (1992: 157–58, 160).

The one story not discussed by either Glenn or Ortega, 'El legado del abuelo', is unquestionably realistic. Like some of the early tales ('Mi hermana Elba', 'El reloj de Bagdad', and 'Los altillos de Brumal'), a first-person narrator deals with childhood experiences from the perspective of the adult. He recalls the death of his grandfather and his mother's frenzied and fruitless search for the old man's oft-mentioned 'treasure', all the while battling with her siblings over the expected inheritance. Gradually, the narrator divulges both that he unintentionally precipitated the old man's death and that he concealed the grandfather's little Chinese box, with its yellowing photos and dirty old pipe. The growing boy convinces himself that the grandfather lied about his hidden wealth to keep his children from rejecting him, and that his only treasure was his family: the figures in the photos. After casting his mother aside – the fate the grandfather had feared for himself – the narrator discovers that the old pipe, inscribed to his mother, is of solid gold.

In the fictional world of Fernández Cubas, family relationships are often problematic and another's death may be seen as a release. In her fantastic tales, this situation is particularly true when one of the characters is rooted in the real and the other's desire leads him or her through the looking glass to an unreal plane of fantasy. There is an implicit adversarial relationship between the protagonist and another. In 'El legado del abuelo', the little boy similarly

disdains the old man, but the tension no longer arises from a collision between real and unreal spheres.

The narrator's attempt over time to decode his grandfather's message, to
decipher the secret of a treasure alluded to but never clarified, has its coun-
terparts in the earlier fantastic and Gothic tales with their frequent references
to indecipherability and the breakdown of communication. Through his
reading of the photographs, the boy at first incorrectly believes that the old
man wanted his grandchild to be the only recipient of his message about the
family. In turn, even after the boy confesses that he has the Chinese box and
describes its contents, the mother dismisses the grimy pipe without looking at
it: '¡Qué tontería! Si el abuelo no había fumado nunca' (88). This very lack
of practical function should have signalled that the pipe was not a pipe, but
something more. When the young man finally discovers the gold and the in-
scription, the words 'Para María Teresa, mi hija' (95) reveal to him the depth
of the old man's unspoken love for his youngest daughter and the boy's own
error in keeping, indeed stealing, the box from his mother.

In another of the stories included in *El ángulo del horror*, 'La Flor de España', the first-person narrator is a Spanish professor who has recently arrived
in an unspecified Scandinavian country. For Bellver (1991: 372), this is the
most realistic work in the collection. Glenn, in my view, is stretching defini-
tions when she finds (1992: 131) that the narrator's presence 'in a foreign
country whose language is "incomprensible"' meets the Gothic requirement
of indecipherability. (If she were right, travel abroad would be more often
equated with nightmares than with cultural enrichment.) In 'La Flor de España', we do not find the genre's familiar spatial aspect: 'Space is always
threatening and never comfortable in the Gothic novel; castles loom with su-
perhuman capacity for entrapment; cloisters induce claustrophobia; rooms
become too small; vistas too grand' (Haggerty 1989: 20). Nor can we say that
'La Flor de España' expresses our innermost fears by articulating 'the dream
of pursuit and escape' (Vincent 1983: 155). And with even less validity can we
think of the narrator as the typical Gothic protagonist, as defined by Ellen
Moers: 'simultaneously persecuted victim and courageous heroine' (quoted in
James 1983: 143). Our unlikely heroine is more persecutor than persecuted.
Bellver is on target when she tells us (1991: 372) that the narrator 'delights in
tormenting the laconic Spanish proprietor of a small delicatessen with obsessive trivial conversation'.

One of Todorov's requirements for the fantastic is a reliable first-person narrator who may lie to other characters but never to us (1970: 87–88). Such a formula avoids ironic distancing between narrator and reader and thus allows for the latter's necessary integration into the former's world. Let me now publicly confess that my 1987 analysis of Fernández Cubas's 'En el hemisferio sur' intentionally passes over the veracity of the male narrator. If he does not lie outright, he does withhold key information, thus distorting our initial understanding of his relationship with the novelist within the story as well as her complete identity. Only after the fact do we realize that he has, or believes he has deliberately precipitated her suicide. In this respect, he is similar to the narrator of 'El legado del abuelo' whose withholding of information likewise creates a retrospective irony of events. 'En el hemisferio sur' is one of Fernández Cubas's most humorous tales and its irony has a wide range of functions. Choosing from the descriptive labels provided by D. C. Muecke (1982: 10), we can ascribe to the narrator an unconscious and self-betraying irony. As he inadvertently shows himself to be petty, envious, and vindictive, the narrator's criticism of the successful novelist's works turns against himself.

The unreliable narrator of 'La Flor de España' also reveals much about herself through unconscious and self-betraying irony. She is prone to misreadings of others and their situations, and her satire of resident Spaniards in a northern land at times boomerangs on herself. Is her rejection of many things Spanish any less objectionable than the others' alleged ethnocentrism? And if she finds the Spaniards' attitudes so offensive, why does she seek out their company and feel impelled to visit the ethnic store, La Flor de España?

The action of 'La Flor de España' takes place over some months. At the outset, the narrator has just been left by her Scandinavian lover, Olav. Then she breaks off her relationship with a second lover, Gert. Later, she is mystified to learn that Olav and Gert have become 'inseparable friends' (152). Finally, she accepts as 'marvellous' the fact that Olav and Gert are lovers (159). The narrator has misread both of the men, failing to discover her lovers' homosexual tendencies. When she first spots the shop window of La Flor de España, she erroneously surmises that the owner is Scandinavian. Even after she enters, sees Rosita, and exchanges a few words with her, she fails to identify the store owner as Spanish. Nor does she display sensitivity in her first interaction with the Spanish colony. Suffering from a well-developed case of foot-in-mouth disease, the narrator initially assumes that her compatriots, who have lived in the city far longer than she, are unaware of La Flor de España's existence and that she is free to speak badly of Rosita to them. Given the narrator's record of failed intuition, why should we believe that she is correct in reading true friendship in the attitude towards her by three of the Spaniards' wives: Gudrun, Ingeborg and Svietta (Scandinavian-sounding names no doubt chosen to amuse the Hispanic reader)?

The central thread of the story, however, is not this aspect of the narrator's presumed integration into an adopted country but rather her adversarial relationship with the owner of La Flor de España. The verbal and psychological warfare between the two has a kind of farcical, even cartoon-like quality, and might be compared to that of cartoon characters Dennis the Menace and Mr Wilson, except that the narrator, while sometimes seemingly naïve, also has a malicious streak. She alternately professes bewilderment and indignation when the owner of the little store does not offer a delivery service or is both too 'indisposed' and too 'busy' to wait on her. The reader, of course, with the benefit of ironic distancing, interprets the series of episodes as Rosita's increasingly desperate efforts to avoid contact with a customer so annoying as to drive the poor shopkeeper mad. Duplicitously or not, the narrator apparently fails to understand that the newly instituted delivery service – which she plans to reject – was invented by the shopkeeper and her friends in an effort to prevent the narrator's visits and thus help Rosita keep her sanity.

The remaining two stories in *El ángulo del horror* hover closer to the unreal but still invite natural, psychological explanations. 'Helicón' is a further example of the author's humorous bent; the first-person narrator conveys self-betraying irony as he recounts the events of the preceding ten days and nine hours. The title story of the collection, quite exceptionally for Fernández Cubas, has a third-person narrator, thus lessening the possibility that the reader will become integrated into the fictional world.

'Helicón', we should recall, is the one tale considered by both Glenn and Ortega, the former under the rubric of Gothic, and the latter as an example of the fantastic. The story centres on a double set of doubles: pairs of real and imaginary twins. As Glenn notes (1992: 137), this 'theme of doubling is treated, initially, in humorous fashion'; whether all readers will agree that it also offers a 'vision of horror' is more debatable. On the other hand, the story is unquestionably related to the kind of metafiction that Patricia Waugh discusses under her category 'role-playing and fictionality as theme' (116 – 19).

In this respect, the story might be compared to such recent Spanish novels as Juan Marsé's *El amante bilingüe* or Luis Landero's *Juegos de la edad tardía*.

The narrator, Marcos, has met an attractive but boring young woman, Ángela, who is obsessed with the subject of twins at all levels, including an aversion to double-yolked eggs. Marcos previously had invented for himself a degenerate twin, Cosme, as a cover-up for his own inexplicable, embarrassing conduct. Eventually, he discovers that the angelic Ángela herself has a real twin, the degenerate Eva. By the end of the tale, Marcos's fictionalized self appears to dominate the 'real' character, when he calls himself Cosme and chooses Eva over Ángela.

The original impetus for the invention of Cosme is a comic-grotesque scene in which the indiscreet Violeta enters Marcos's apartment unannounced and finds the dishevelled, nude, sweaty man surrounded by disgusting filth and disarray, playing his helicon (a kind of coiled tuba, akin to a sousaphone). Ortega (1992: 157) attributes Marcos's 'descent into hell' to the helicon, source of the fantastic. I am more inclined to attribute his decadent state to alcohol, for Marcos has all the hallmarks of a binge drinker. While Ángela drones on about twins, he downs 'whisky tras whisky' (22); at the time of Violeta's discovery, 'la cerveza discurría por mi pecho' (28). Considering how unpopular his tuba concerts must be with his neighbours, he doubtless has to be drunk before indulging in his musical interludes.

The state of Marcos's apartment and his person is not dissimilar to that of the narrator in 'Los altillos de Brumal' just before she elects to return to the unreal world; she, too, is suspected of alcoholism. But in 'Helicón', Todorov's requisite doubt is absent. At no time does the narrator suggest that the tuba controls him, nor is he confused about a possible, separate existence of Cosme. Cosme may be the suppressed, unacceptable side of Marcos's personality, but we do not have to probe beneath the surface of the fantastic to uncover this psychoanalytic interpretation.

In 'El ángulo del horror', the third-person narration is focused through the perspective of Julia, a young girl whose eighteen-year old brother Carlos has become taciturn and shut himself away in an attic room of the family's summer home. Carlos eventually tells his sister of a dream in which he had seen himself, outside this very house, viewing it from a new angle. The residual sense of horror from the dream leads to his suicide, and the image of her dead brother in turn drives Julia, through a process of empathy, to assume his angle of vision. She sees her own, increasingly horrified image, mirrored first in her brother's dark glasses and then in her little sister's frightened eyes.

José Ortega accurately equates 'El ángulo del horror' with a vision of death (1992: 160–61), but the choice of narrative perspective removes this tale from the fantastic mode. On this point, a comparison with 'La mujer de verde', a story included in *Con Ágatha en Estambul*, is illuminating.

In Fernández Cubas's earlier tales, deaths occur as part of the story line ('Lúnula y Violeta', 'Mi hermana Elba', and 'En el hemisferio sur'). In two of the most recent tales, 'La mujer de verde' and 'El lugar', death becomes the central theme. In the first of these, the story clearly meets all of Todorov's requirements for the fantastic mode. The second tale straddles the fantastic and the uncanny.

In 'La mujer de verde', no overt, rational explanation is ever provided for the apparition that haunts the first-person narrator, a professional woman who has been leading a double life as her boss's respected assistant and as his lover. In his absence, the narrator begins to exploit a new employee, Dina Dachs, whom she overworks mercilessly. She also is obsessed with the idea that she sees Dina –wearing a green silk dress with a purple collar– in the most unlikely places. Over the several days of sightings, the mental state of the narrator deteriorates, as does the image of the Dina look-alike until the latter turns into a beggar. Finally, in a nightmare-like confrontation in a dead-end street, the narrator perceives that the woman in green is Death. The narrator interprets the vision as meaning that Dina's life is in danger and goes to warn the younger woman who, working late on Christmas Eve, is already wearing a green silk party dress for later that evening. The narrator strangles Dina, encircling her neck in purplish bruises. In a passage written in the future tense, we learn that only after the body and the young woman's letters are discovered, will the narrator and reader learn that Dina is the boss's new lover and that she has dared to express in her letters the very words that the narrator has only thought about regarding her own desires.

Among the positive reviews of *Con Ágatha en Estambul* published in Spain are these insightful comments about 'La mujer de verde': it is 'un relato de desdoblamiento, de locura y de terror, drama de destrucción y autodestrucción' (Masoliver Ródenas); 'es el descubrimiento minucioso de un proceso de locura del que el personaje parece estar ajeno' (Botana). It is precisely because the narrator does not fully understand her deteriorating mental state and that both she and the reader vacillate between accepting the woman in green as real and rejecting her as a hallucination that the story remains clearly within the realm of the fantastic. Yes, the narrator is ill: she resorts to sleeping pills and knows that Dina, at least, must think she is mad. Although the thought is never expressed, she may indeed have intuited that the boss had his special reasons for hiring Dina.[3] But how did she know about the green silk dress? And how do we explain Dina's text that puts into writing the narrator's thoughts, verbatim?

By contrast, in 'El ángulo de horror' we do not have the opportunity to deal with such unanswered questions and ambiguities. The narration is focused through Julia's perspective and we are never inside Carlos's head. He does recount his dream, but dreams, as an expression of the unconscious, may readily be given a psychoanalytic, rather than supernatural interpretation. Moreover, while we do not know what triggered Carlos's death instinct, we do know that Julia's sense of horror stems, first, from her glimpse into Carlos's disturbed, inner world and, then, from the sight of her dead brother.

Like 'El ángulo del horror', 'El lugar' deals with the death fixation and dreams of two characters: directly, with respect to the first-person narrator, and indirectly, through what he tells of his wife, Clarisa. The action takes place over a number of years, starting from a few hours after their wedding to some months after the wife's death. From the moment Clarisa first visits the narrator's family mausoleum, she is convinced that there is life within the pantheon, asks to be buried there, and directs her attention to the great beyond.

Without a narration from Clarisa's perspective, the reader has no evidence that the unreal has entered her life, luring her to her death. The narrator's subsequent obsession, readily understandable in psychological terms, does not take the form of supernatural apparitions. In countless literary works, the beloved person's spirit returns visually, if not physically, to be with the one left behind. (Recent examples, easily accessible to Fernández Cubas, include José Sanchis Sinisterra's 1986 hit play, *¡Ay, Carmela!*, the 1986 Carlos Saura-Antonio Gades film, *El amor brujo*, and the 1990 American film, *Ghost* (entitled *Más allá del amor* for distribution in Spain). Clarisa's ghost, on the other hand, remains on the level of dream fantasy. From the earliest days of

---

3. The story exemplifies Lacan's concept of 'repudiation': 'that which has not been admitted to symbolic expression ('repudiated') reappears in reality in the form of hallucination': Laplanche & Pontalis (1986: 30).

Freudian analysis, unconscious desires have been said to be played out in dreams as if in the 'private theatre' of the mind (Laplanche & Pontalis 1986: 5). This is precisely the analogy verbalized in the tale:

> Pero al rato, aguzando el oído, me pareció percibir algunos susurros, ciertos bisbiseos, como si me hallara en el patio de butacas de un teatro, y los actores, no muy diestros desde luego, se aprestaran a ocupar sus puestos.

(144)

The narrator's obsessive dreams about his dead wife and her experiences in the afterlife gradually become independent of the dreamer. In 'El ángulo del horror', Carlos and his two sisters are all aware of being able to control their dreams, of being able to change their situation even in a nightmare: 'Ella (Julia), y sólo ella, era la dueña absoluta de aquella mágica sucesión de imágenes' (107). The narrator in 'El lugar' initially has but then loses this capacity: 'Era la primera vez que el sueño se desmandaba, cobraba vida propia y lograba sorprenderme. Hasta entonces –y sólo ahora me daba cuenta– Clarisa se había limitado a pronunciar frases esperadas, plausibles, tópicas' (137). Clarisa's comments have ironically debunked the family legends that the narrator earlier related, but they are at least based on his script. Less open to rational explanation is his imagining of a scene that will later take place, almost exactly, when he draws up his will and takes it to the doctor who attended Clarisa in her illness. The narrator's planning for his own death, including gifts for Clarisa that he will have buried with him, is triggered by a last performance in the theatre of his mind in which his mother intervenes, speaking to him as if he were a child: 'Hijo, por favor, no insistas. ¿No ves que Clarisa está ocupada?' (146).

According to Ayala-Dip in his review of *Con Ágatha en Estambul* for *El País*, 'El lugar', with its 'tono crepuscular', is reminiscent of Henry James's *The Altar of the Dead*. In 'Ausencia', a narration in second person, he finds a relationship with Carlos Fuentes's *Aura*. In these four works, he affirms that fate holds for the heroines 'experiencias incomunicables. No tropiezan con ellas, se cruzan premeditadamente'. Perhaps, and perhaps not. 'Ausencia' deals with a case of temporary amnesia. Again, we need not resort to supernatural explanations for the event; what we certainly do have here is a splendid defamiliarization of the life of a successful professional woman.

Elena Vila Gastón, the amnesia victim in 'Ausencia', turns out to be a magazine editor who has achieved everything she dreamed of as a little girl.

In the gradual process of self-identification, as she follows the clues to her name, address, age, native language, occupation, and sentimental attachments, she concludes that she is or ought to be enormously happy. But, as Alicia Botana astutely observes, Elena's momentary loss of memory 'se transforma en una meditación sobre la insatisfacción de las mujeres, ese desasosiego inhóspito con que ellas suelen convivir, encontrando ventura sólo allí donde no están, sólo allí donde no son' (1994: unpaginated). When the editor returns to her job, her friendly tone of voice quickly reverts to her usual ill-humoured one. The stress of her daily routine wipes out the euphoria caused by the previous day's process of defamiliarization.

In general, Fernández Cubas's female protagonists are not happy, friendly, well adjusted people. But in analysing her representation of women, we must not overlook her habitual use of humour and irony. 'La ausencia', for example, is filled with deliciously comic moments. The second-person narrator invents for Elena a series of hypothetical dialogues that, of course, never take place. When she calls her phone number, ready to leave a message with a servant, she finds only her own voice on the answering machine. When she knocks at the door, prepared to explain the reason for her visit, no one answers; she opens with the key she finds in the purse that must be hers because it matches the shoes she is wearing. On the way to the apartment, she stops in church and makes confession, starting with the litany of childish sins that she probably mentioned the last time she went. She quickly improvises more adult sins, including a bank robbery, and then imitates an answering machine message. The priest, no doubt deaf, makes no response.

The remaining two stories in *Con Ágatha en Estambul* also have first-person female narrators. The action of 'El mundo' takes place in a convent over a long period of years. The title story in the collection revolves around the narrator's unhappy Christmas trip to Turkey with her husband and has, as an intertext, an episode of temporary amnesia suffered by Agatha Christie.

Newspaper reviews of *Con Ágatha en Estambul* by Botana and Masoliver Ródenas take diametrically opposite stances on the enclosed world of the convent in 'El mundo'. For the former (1994), there is an 'elemento amenazador' and the story 'retrata el oprimente ambiente de un convento donde una niña es abandonada por un padre indiferente y falaz, sin más señas de identidad que un baúl de caoba en cuyos cajoncitos secretos atesora sus rencores y decepciones'. For the latter (1994), this same story is 'el más encantador', precisely because of 'el aura mágica del convento, el humour, lo mara-villoso, la acumulación de sorpresas y la ingenuidad'. Although Botana has captured surface elements of the story, Masoliver Ródenas seems to me to provide a more accurate assessment of the tone than Botana. The narrator of 'El mundo' accepts convent life and has no desire to return to the secular world she has left outside the walls; like the protagonist of 'Los altillos de Brumal', she willingly rejects freedom for enclosure.

The 'mundo' that the narrator brings with her is an old trunk; along with the wedding dress of her mother, who died when the narrator was born, it rep-resents her matrilineal heritage. As Botana says, the young girl uses the many compartments of the trunk as places to store away mentally the subjects that most distress her. The physical trunk itself is marked by fascinating images, most specifically that of a sailor standing with his back to a sailing vessel and holding a picture of a sailor standing with his back to a sailing vessel, who, in turn, holds a picture, and so on. Eventually Carolina will destroy the infinite regression of carvings on the trunk with their message of freedom represented by the sailing vessel.

Inheritance, in a materialistic sense, and particularly the family conflicts to which it gives rise, is a repeated theme in Fernández Cubas's stories ('Los al-tillos de Brumal', 'El legado del abuelo', 'El lugar'). In the case of 'El mundo', the young girl sent away to the convent has no knowledge for many years that her 'punishment' was a means for her father to steal the money that was rightfully hers. Although she reveals the information only gradually, she is far more aware of the sexual explanations for her becoming a nun. In a kind of primal scene, she had witnessed the physical relationship first of her father and, later, of the priest, both with the servant Eulalia. The priest, to protect himself from the young girl's stories, had invented his own story, about her supposed amorous fling with a boy, as a justification for shutting her away.

While the reasons for Carolina's enclosure in the convent are not without literary precedent, the depiction of the nuns' world, although not so wild as Pedro Almodóvar's unorthodox convent in the 1983 film *Entre tinieblas*, never-theless is innovative. It ranges from the conflict between the sisters' elegant needlework and the post-war infatuation with nylon which took away their livelihood, to legends about a self-sacrificing nun long ago who starved herself to feed stray cats and about another, contemporary one, who kills stray cats as a way of earning money for the convent. Story-telling and the reading of unusual texts is highlighted with the arrival of a supposedly mute nun from Peru who communicates through carved gourds and pumpkins. The narrator, reflecting Fernández Cubas's typical irony, is proud of her ability to speak for the mute sister and to interpret her pictorial writings which, like the carvings on the trunk, are presented ecphrastically to the reader. Eventually the mysterious sister proves to be neither mute nor Peruvian, but rather – partially mirroring Carolina's own story – someone who has seen a crime and has taken refuge in convents, silence, and home-made pumpkin wine, as a way to escape. When Interpol takes Mother Peru away, her pumpkin masterpiece depicting this convent's legends mysteriously disappears. In truth, it is the narrator herself who has taken retaliation for a perceived betrayal. Like many of Fernández Cubas's protagonists, Carolina has read both the text (the pumpkin carving) and its author incorrectly and, with self-betraying irony, establishes that she is capable of petty, destructive vengeance.

The narrator of 'Con Ágatha en Estambul' shares a number of character defects and humiliations with protagonists from other stories. This is a rich tale, incorporating many of Fernández Cubas's favourite devices, particularly metafictional ones. When the forty-year old narrator and her husband Julio, to whom she has been married for fifteen years, arrive in Istanbul for a fifteen-day Christmas vacation, the city is so shrouded in mysterious fog that it seems unreal. Also unreal is the narrator's sudden and surprising ability to speak Turkish. While these clues might lead us to expect another fantastic tale, in fact they are planted playfully. When the jealous narrator flees back to Barcelona, leaving Julio behind with his new friend Flora, the sun finally comes out, dispelling the mists and revealing the city's landmarks. Moreover, the narrator's knowledge of Turkish reaches a plateau in lesson seven of her manual, and she is chagrined to discover that she only half understood what her acquaintances – the shoeshine boy, the taxi-driver, and the travel agent – have been telling her.

Typical of Fernández Cubas's protagonists, who are often the ironic butt of their own plotting or efforts at story-telling, the narrator is prone to inventing fictions and hence to misreading others' texts. Her immediate hostility to Flora, a compatriot who has seemingly been abandoned by her travel companions, only precipitates her husband's involvement with the woman. Around Flora she weaves stories that might have been written by Agatha Christie herself, and the final showdown with Julio has all the melodramatic overtones of a performance by Sarah Bernhardt: Istanbul's Pera Palas, where they are staying, has rooms named after both famous personages, and the narrator's interaction with them informs the tale.

The narrator convinces herself that a fish in the restaurant aquarium – reminiscent of Julio Cortázar's story 'Axolotl' – can speak to her and take on human form. Like Clara's double in 'En el hemisferio sur', she hears her own voice offering her advice. And she persuades herself that Agatha is still up in room 411. She associates the mystery writer's inexplicable disappearance and case of amnesia with marital problems and reminds herself that Christie later remarried and found true happiness. The narrator does not vanish in the same way but, while inebriated, she slips and develops a grotesquely swollen ankle that leaves her unable to accompany her husband on his tourist travels. Their days of separation thus function in parodic parallel to Agatha's disappearance and lead to a parallel breakdown in their marriages.

While the various voices and ghosts that speak to the narrator might be construed as fantastic elements, the story remains on a more realistic and ironic level. In her lonely strolls through the Turkish bazaar, she buys a bottle of cheap perfume that purports to be Chanel's 'Égoïste'. Egotistically, she pours on the foul-smelling stuff, first forcing Julio to open the taxi window in the frigid December air and then acquiring three seats to herself on the plane home when the passenger next to her moves away. The narrator's lack of sensitivity to others results in humorous scenes that subvert any sympathetic reading that we might otherwise give her as the victim of some malevolent force. This narrator, like many others of Fernández Cubas's characters, is so immersed in self and so prone to imagination that she brings disaster upon herself and those around her.

It has not been my purpose here to negate the fantastic elements in many of Fernández Cubas's tales, but rather to point out that there are other aspects of her work worthy of study. Serving as links between her fantastic and her realistic stories are innovative uses of metafiction, probing psychological analysis, and finely honed irony. The rich world of Cristina Fernández Cubas is one that invites varied readings and scholarly analysis.

PHYLLIS ZATLIN

Rutgers, The State University of New Jersey

MARIA SANZ'S LANDSCAPES WITH SOUL:
A WOMAN'S VISION

El alma del poeta
se orienta hacia el misterio.
Sólo el poeta puede
mirar lo que está lejos
dentro del alma, en turbio
y mago sol envuelto.

(Machado 1952: 68)

IN A RECENT STUDY of the use of evocation in twentieth-century Spanish literature by men and women (Ciplijauskaité 1993), I came to the conclusion that male authors are usually more egocentric, the images they create more dynamic, and the separation between past and present more complete. That investigation was based principally on contemporary psychological experiments, and at least a portion of the male writing seemed to conform to the postmodern canon. In this essay I propose to examine certain processes in the creation of landscapes by María Sanz, without attempting to prove that a woman's perception necessarily works differently from that of a man.[1] As a matter of fact, apart from undeniable – maybe unconscious – affinities with María Victoria Atencia's attitudes and creative strategies, María Sanz comes closest in her landscapes to Antonio Machado's 'paisajes con alma' – with the variant that his 'tierras pobres, tierras tristes, | tan tristes que tienen alma' become 'tan bellas que tienen alma' – which leads us back to Bécquer. A Sevillian, like Machado, she fits better into the parameters of modernism than postmodernism. Bachelard's theories on creative imagination and Merleau-Ponty's and Husserl's phenomenology of perception offer the most helpful in-

---

1. María Sanz was born in 1956 in Seville, where she continues to live, and after finishing secondary education started to work as an administrative assistant. Since 1981, she has published ten books of poetry, nine of which have received prizes. She has also written a novel, *Las mujeres de Don Juan* (1989).

sights for the analysis of her work which, according to her own declaration, strives to be 'intimista' and highlights transcendence achieved through the contemplation of beauty (Ugalde 1991: 205, 209).[2]

Discussing postmodern art, Richard Kearney suggests that 'the suspension of subjective inwardness, referential depth, historical time, and coherent human expression... is now becoming *de rigueur*' (1988: 5). María Sanz, on the contrary, presents a clear line and great unity in every one of her ten books of poetry: 'hay que tener siempre un sentido y una orientación' (Ugalde 1991: 205). Subjective inwardness is a salient characteristic of her poetic universe. While the postmodern artist emphasizes images as artefacts which 'have now replaced the "original" realities they were traditionally meant to reflect' and represent only 'a trick of hyperrealist technique' (Kearney 1988: 2, 12) which is to be recognized as such, María Sanz's ideal is to produce 'serene, limpid, open' poetry that enables identification and compenetration (Ugalde 1991: 205). In this, she coincides with Bachelard: 'La première tâche du poète est de désancrer en nous une matière qui veut rêver' (1943: 217).[3] Hers is not a play with proliferating images in the mode of a collage but a self-generating cultural-historical context inherent in a coherent portrait of the inner self. Ortega y Gasset's characterization of Antonio Machado's *Campos de Castilla* outlines the process perceptively:

> Nótese que no estriba el acierto en que los alcores se califiquen de cárdenos ni la tierra de parda. Estos adjetivos de colores se limitan a proporcionarnos como el mínimo aparato alucinatorio que nos es forzoso para que actualicemos, para que nos pongamos delante una realidad más profunda, poética, y sólo poética... Esta fuerte imagen subyacente da

---

2.   For a full discussion of these theories consult Richard Kearney (1991). Bachelard posits imagination as an intentionality of self-transcendence and underscores the quality of remaining open, perceiving anew with every contact, a palimpsest-like growth in constant interaction between the imagining subject and the created image which surpasses reality (called 'the invisible' by Merleau-Ponty). He insists on primary oneiric experience, which permits the abolition of the barrier between self and other: the imagining subject becomes a 'more-than-I'. Merleau-Ponty, speaking of the perception of landscape, posits the relation of equal to equal between the contemplating subject and the contemplated object and specifies that perception is not an exclusively sensorial experience: it is the subsequent reflection that sets in motion the creative act. Husserl also insists on the potential element. Things are apprehended in their essence when they are grasped not only in their actuality but also in their possibility. All three underscore 'intuitive essence'.

3.   The 'serene, limpid, open' calls to mind Bachelard's 'l'homme reconcilié' achieved through free flight of the poetic imagination.

humana reviviscencia a todo el paisaje y provee de nervios vivaces, de
aliento y de personalidad, a la pobre realidad inerte de la cárdena y parda
gleba.

(1912: 279)

This corresponds with Husserl's intentional consciousness and Bachelard's
and Merleau-Ponty's reflections on perception: not fixation of a given, but
elaboration of a possibility. In more than one way, Sanz's poetry responds to
treatises on the poetic imagination and poetic creation that circulated in Spain
in the first part of the century, like Max Scheler's *Ordo amoris*, which inspired
María Zambrano's 'Hacia un saber sobre el alma', or Ortega y Gasset's
'Vitalidad, alma, espíritu', and shows surprisingly close points of contact with
Zambrano's 'La metáfora del corazón'.

The world María Sanz presents is not described; it is intuitively suggested.
Bachelard explains this phenomenon, stating that the task of imagination is to
distort images furnished by sensorial perception, enriching the seen with the
unseen and thereby creating a special tension (1943: 7–11). He also suggests
that 'la manière dont nous nous échappons du réel désigne nettement notre
réalité intime' (14). This is well illustrated by the example he gives of the image of a bird's flight. The most aerial, most frequently sung bird is the lark,
whose colours the eye does not perceive; it is the impetus of soaring to the
sky united with the song that matters. The most earthbound bird is the pea-
cock, whose rich plumage distracts from a possible plus-being (he never flies).
María Sanz's poetic universe is peopled by the imperceptible fluttering of
wings: flight and upward movement are frequent in her verse and expected to
generate a reciprocal sensation in the reader, approaching Novalis's precept
of *Gemütserregungskunst* – the art of arousing emotion (Bachelard 1943: 218).
She herself has indicated the poems 'Alas' and 'Clausura' as most representative of her poetic world, whose motion is so well defined by Zambrano:

> El corazón es el símbolo y representación máxima de todas las entrañas
> de la vida, la entraña donde todas encuentran su unidad definitiva, y su
> nobleza... lleva consigo la imagen de un espacio, de un *dentro* obscuro,
> secreto y misterioso que, en ocasiones, se abre. Este abrirse es su mayor
> nobleza... Aquello que primariamente es sólo pasividad – acusación– se
> transforma en activo. Interioridad que se ofrece para seguir siendo inte-
> rioridad, sin anularla.

(1950c: 46)

A constant closely related to this preference for closed inner space is vagueness: 'lo nebuloso que me gusta siempre (Ugalde 1991: 211). From the very first book it is associated with the intuition of possibilities into which one may read an echo of Husserl's theory of imagination (things are apprehended in their essence when they are grasped not only in their actual presence but also in their potential; imagination helps to disclose meaning by intuition):

> Lejos, muy lejos, alma, te pareces
> tal vez a un resplandor desconocido.

(Sanz 1991b: 13)

Not only does this indeterminacy leave a greater margin for the imagination; according to Sanz, it also establishes a kind of protective screen. It permits the perception of the ever-changing contours of a second-degree reality. Bachelard sees indeterminacy as the epitome of the creative moment: 'L'âme qui rêve devant le nuage léger reçoit à la fois l'image matérielle d'une effusion et l'image dynamique d'une ascension' (1943: 220). It leads to a sense of plenitude, to 'absolute sublimation' since it enables the transcendence of temporality (Zambrano 1971: 144).[4]

*   *   *   *   *

THE VOLUME OF María Sanz's poetry is already considerable, as are the prizes she has been garnering since 1981. There is also growing interest in her work among the critics. For this brief study I shall limit myself to one type of poem only: the portrayal of a landscape. In such poems, the blending of exterior and interior worlds is complete and, without entering explicitly, or doing so just in the last line, the poet incorporates her most intimate 'I'. Her procedures remind us of Atencia's Venetian and Florentine gems, where perceived reality is displaced by the reflection it provokes, followed by emotional fusion.

The reflections are different in the two poets: more elaborate, more 'cultural' (she writes at the time of the Novísimos), more centered around the perceiving subject, and predominantly affective in Atencia; springing forth from more objective presentation, followed by subsequent immersion in Sanz. This is clear from the following two poems:

---

4.   Zambrano uses similar words to define it: 'Queda entonces la realidad suspendida, absolutizada, en estado de ser' (1971: 23).

PLACETA DE SAN MARCOS

Amárrate, alma mía; sujétate a este mármol,
Sebastián de su tronco, con cuantas cintas pueda
ofrecerte en Venecia la lluvia que te empapa.

Amárrate a este palo, alma Ulises, y escucha
–desde donde la plaza proclama su equilibrio–
el rugido de bronce que la piedra sostiene.

(Atencia 1990: 107)

LA LUZ DE SU MILAGRO

Los muros acogían bellamente
las transparencias místicas de *I Frari* :
recoleta portada, campanario
románico. Y adentro, las cenizas
de Tiziano, quien quiso que su *Assunta*,
arrebatada de entre los Apóstoles,
mostrara en aquel éxtasis el tiempo
de llegar hasta Dios... Quedó la iglesia
tan nítida a la luz de su milagro,
que no advertí el claror de la mañana.

(Sanz 1991b: 17)

The perceiving subject, very much in the manner of Heidegger or Husserl,
remains awestruck in wonder.[5] In Atencia, marvel is present from the very
first line; Sanz renders the birth of emotion gradually. The density and the
power of suggestion achieved by means of ellipsis are greater in Atencia; also
more noticeable is the use of stylistic devices (rhythmic repetition, alliteration,
final metaphor). All is geared to the effect the place produces on the speaking 'I' and also, by transference, on the reader. Sanz begins in an almost narrative tone, but she narrates a mystery produced by art which is then transformed into light on two levels. There is very little description. What matters
is the meaning of the elements enumerated. She literally names the miracle

---

5.   Both Husserl and Heidegger use the expression, insisting that there is more than the
sensorial perception of the world which we find ourselves 'thrown into'. There remains an
inexplicable side to all this. Our perception is helped by intuition which is momentaneous,
hence susceptible to change, and produces another revelation that inspires the awe and marvel
that forms the basis of every work of art.

and, through the structure, permits the reader to *sense* 'el tiempo | de llegar hasta Dios'. Represented and experienced miracle are fused.

In the end, in both poems the 'I' is obliterated: in one, all becomes vibration of a sound – 'c'est la partie *vibrante* de notre être qui peut connaître l'alouette' (Bachelard 1943: 101); in the other, it is 'la luz y la visión, pero referidas a otro órgano distinto del pensamiento... el corazón' (Zambrano 1950c: 43). In both, 'lenguaje sagrado' (Zambrano 1950a: 33) is at work, and this places them within the modernist tradition and phenomenological imagination. Words become dynamic and are transformed into 'fórmulas que hacen abrirse un espacio antes inaccesible' (33). In both poems, we are offered an *Erlebnis* (lived experience). In both, the perceiving subject abstracts herself from observed reality and superimposes on it another reality, which comes close to the phenomenon described by Zambrano as day-dreaming:

> La realidad se desvanece o se oculta, y el sujeto se queda ciego ante ella... Queda entonces la realidad suspendida... La acción verdadera que los sueños de la persona proponen es un despertar del íntimo fondo de la persona o ese fondo inasible desde el cual la persona es, si no una máscara, sí una figura que puede deshacerse y rehacerse; un despertar trascendente.
>
> (1971: 22, 23, 39)

Bachelard (1943: 80) specifies that this rapture is always translated into movement: 'dans l'instant où l'être émerveillé vit son étonnement, il fait abstraction de tout un univers, au profit d'un trait de feu, d'un mouvement qui chante'. The insistence on movement that sings ought not to be forgotten: in a declaration about her working habits, María Sanz underscores that music is actually even more important to her than poetry, and that she always writes following a rhythm. The Orphic origin of poetry was a frequent theme among neo-symbolists. Zambrano traces it back to the cult of Dionysus, emphasizing another element almost always present in Sanz's verse: Nature – 'el alma busca a la naturaleza en lo que tiene de musical, de ímpetu clarificado. Es un baño cósmico, una reconciliación del alma con la vida' (1950b: 21).

In relation with this capacity to fuse with Nature, it might be interesting to remember the difference Bachelard, in his good-natured patriarchal attitude, establishes between dream, which he deems male, and day-dream, an 'essentially feminine activity'. He attributes dream to *animus*, day-dream to *anima*, and points out that men love things and dream about them with a view to using them, whereas women love things 'intimement, pour elles-mêmes, avec les lenteurs du féminin' (1971: 27). Therefore, he posits, their day-dreams bring a sense of great tranquillity: 'le véritable repos', which can be sensed in both poems we have seen. The barrier between 'I' and 'the other' disappears: 'Dans la rêverie, il n'y a plus de non-moi... Tout est acceuil' (1971: 144). This is what occurs in another poem by Atencia:

> voy pisando y me oigo
> y soy mi propio eco y mi propia cautela
> hasta que te me abres, belleza desmedida
> que abarco en mi pañuelo.

(Atencia 1990: 277)

Such opening-up confers on the perceiver 'un plus-être' (Bachelard 1971: 131).[6] It is the 'stepping out of intimacy without leaving it' of which Zambrano talks. In both Atencia and Sanz imagination is as important as perception: the contemplated object changes constantly. For Husserl, imagination is 'an indispensable agency for the disclosure and intuition of meaning' (Kearney 1991: 20).[7] Both poets do just that: they tell us what the object of the poem means to them at that particular time, and thereby transmit what Husserl calls *Wesensschau*, or the intuition of ideal essences.[8]

*   *   *   *   *

MARÍA SANZ'S most original poems born from contemplating a landscape form the first part of *Los aparecidos*. There are only ten of them, but they suffice to enter her name among the most interesting practitioners of this art.

---

6.   Compare Merleau-Ponty: 'Le monde est non pas ce que je pense, mais ce que je vis, je suis ouvert au monde ... il est inépuisable' (1945: xii). He comes close to describing the process experienced in the two poems: 'voir jaillir d'une constellation de données un sens immanent' (30). Women are deemed to be particularly deft in opening temporal limits: 'It is this evocative power of images that defines the feminine approach to perception' (Martin 1988: 41).

7.   'It is in this shift of attention from the empirical existence of things, as objects among objects, to their intentional existence, as live phenomena of consciousness, that imagination is accredited as the surest means of grasping essences. In other words, imagination releases things from their contingent status as facts and grants them an ideal status as possibilities, possibilities of which each fact is but a single instance' (Kearney 1991: 21).

8.   A good example of the phenomenological approach is 'Cuenca', where the object is reduced to possibility, and the image represents genesis, not effect (Kearney 1991: 91): 'Ya no sé si te alumbro en un poema | o si oscurezco el aura de tu nombre | ... | ya no sé si estás hecha desde siempre | o si te das a luz a cada instante' (Sanz 1991a: 19–20).

They do not follow the same pattern, but are all based on profound compenetration.[9] Each poem represents an experience in which fusion of different temporal levels is possible, as exemplified in an earlier poem from *Cenáculo Vinciano*:

> Al llegar a Florencia, se entrelazan
> luminosos recuerdos con vivencias
> de cercana ebriedad.
>
> ...
>
> Quiero aquí bajar mis ojos
> al húmedo cristal donde se funden
> un escorzo, una cúpula, un ducado.

(Sanz 1986: 224)

One might try to find feminine characteristics in her mode of perception and presentation. She herself specifies that she does not object to the adjective if it is to stand for 'delicate' (Ugalde 1991: 207). She is quite explicit about the emotional component: 'No me gusta que una escritora por compararse al hombre intente quitar de la mente su sentimiento femenino' (207).

The first poem of the group, 'Numantia', does not, contrary to expectations, emphasize action, nor does it exalt the inhabitants' heroic fight. It does not even mention the ruins. All historical data are taken for granted in the reader's memory. Sanz's feminine sensibility (less inclined to closure and stretching out to give: Bachelard 1971: 27) chooses to speak of life rather than death. The first stanza offers scattered notes of everyday occupations:

> Así es la vida aquí: cantan los pájaros,
> se oyen ecos de alfares,
> de andanzas y faenas
> pastoriles.

The second and last achieves the effect by repetition and contrast, adding a note of precision to the 'cualquier presagio oscuro' of the first:

> Así es la vida aquí. Corre el verano
> del 133 antes de Cristo,

---

9. Again, Merleau-Ponty (1945: 82) offers a very precise formulation of the process: 'Regarder un objet, c'est venir l'habiter et de là saisir toutes choses selon la face qu'elles tournent vers lui. Mais, dans la mesure où je les vois elles aussi, elles restent des demeures ouvertes à mon regard, et situé virtuellement en elles, j'aperçois déjà sous différents angles l'objet central de ma vision actuelle. Ainsi chaque objet est le miroir de tous les autres.'

y también el rumor de que se acerca
Escipión con sus tropas.

(Sanz 1991a: 11)

The rest is left to the reader's imagination. The 'I' does not enter. It only creates the necessary tension by substituting observed reality with a suggestion of impending destruction. Two views of Numancia: a healthy little town depicted in a few lines; an unnamed ruin every Spaniard carries in her or his mind. Between the two, the real development of the poem, without words. As Bachelard defines it (1943: 11): 'Le mobilisme *imaginé* n'est pas bien alerté par la description d'un devenir du réel. Le vrai voyage de l'imagination c'est le voyage au pays de l'imaginaire.' Even more important is the note he adds (16) about the affective element: 'Seule une sympathie pour une matière peut déterminer une participation réellement active.' The effect the poem produces fits well into his description of poetry as 'le premier phénomène du silence. Elle laisse vivant, sous les images, le silence attentif' (282).

Even more 'unrealistic' – but again, demonstrating a capacity of feeling – is 'El Espino'. This four-liner is a true palimpsest. There is no real landscape: any student of Spanish poetry knows what El Espino represents. The name immediately calls to mind one of Machado's most nostalgic poems, 'A José María Palacio', whose last four lines represent the starting point for Sanz:

Con los primeros lirios
y las primeras rosas de las huertas,
en una tarde azul, sube al Espino,
al alto Espino donde está su tierra.

(Machado 1952: 154)

Machado does not name the real subject: he was a master, as Claudio Guillén has shown (1957), of 'estilística del silencio'. Sanz picks up the sensation and gives us, standing at the site, her version of it:

Una estrella pronuncia tu nombre cada noche
en este fiel silencio, Leonor. Cuántas palabras
callaría el poeta, sabiendo que tal brillo
iba a ser eco eterno de su pena allá arriba.

(1991a: 13)

The name El Espino has become inseparably united with the figure of Machado who was evoking the presence of Leonor without naming her. Sanz, on the contrary, introduces the only total caesura in order to underscore the name. No description is called for: as in ancient myths, even the grief has been transposed, emphasizing it by strategic placement of corresponding words: 'estrella', 'brillo', 'eterno', 'arriba'.[10] Even more striking is the emphasis on the theme of silence practised by both Machado and Sanz: 'cuántas palabras callaría el poeta' suggests that authentic feeling cannot be rendered in words but also that true emotions originate in silence.[11] It is in poems like this that one understands Bachelard's affirmation that 'c'est la partie *vibrante* de notre être qui peut connaître l'alouette' (1943: 101): contagion through emotion, not through a clearly delineated image.

Every one of these *estampas* is a dialogue with the spirit of the place evoked, which, through this contact, continues to grow but also to become more abstract. Thus, in 'Calatañazor', the first stanza offers a few external details which are synthesized in the first line of the second stanza: 'Pueblo oscuro'. In the last lines, the place has become completely internalized:

> Pueblo escondido en mi memoria, tiemblas
> cada vez que acaricio tu misterio.

> > (Sanz 1991a: 15)

Zambrano explains this process well: 'Lo que es real en el soñar no son las historias y figuraciones, sino el movimiento íntimo del sujeto bajo la atemporalidad' (1971: 44). This applies also to 'Almazán', where several historical allusions are made first, and the last lines are again lifted out of time:

> Por tantos seculares
> designios – cerros, torres,
> callejas y palacios –,
> te rindes, Almazán, a tu belleza.

> > (Sanz 1981a: 16)

The last poem to be discussed is 'Ordesa'. Again, previous knowledge of the place will help to capture the unsaid. As in the others, there is little precision of details which have been transcended. In an interview, Sanz has confessed that the two women poets she admires most are Rosalía de Castro, for 'esa capacidad de captar la tristeza', and St Teresa of Avila, for her 'luz

---

10. Would it be proper to see here a reminiscence of Ariadne's crown converted into a constellation so that her pain may for ever shine in the sky?

11. 'Me impone mucho el silencio. He estado en el campo, sobre todo en Castilla, que es para mí una región silenciosa por excelencia, y me ha llegado a impresionar' (Ugalde 1991: 210).

interior' that permits penetration of the great mysteries. In 'Ordesa' we have
a complete merging of subject and object, which might remind us of Salinas's

> ¡Ay, cómo quisiera ser
> arena, sol, en estío!
> Que te tendieses descansada a descansar.
> . . .
> ¡Ay, cómo quisiera ser
> vidrio, o estofa o madera
> que conserva su color
> aquí...!

(Salinas 1971: 259)

except that, even in this attitude of the perfect *siervo de amor*, there remains
some vested interest: he is yearning for a trace of the beloved's physical contact. There is still separation. In Sanz's case the union is complete.[12] The
stance she adopts reminds us of the distinction Bachelard makes between
masculine and feminine. In her poem we find love of the elements for their
own sake, a constant desire to give:

> Después de haberme convertido en ave
> y abrazar estas cumbres con un vuelo
> sosegado; tras ser la nieve rosa
> que habitan los crepúsculos, rizándome
> en cada manantial; cuando ha corrido
> mi cuerpo cristalino por un cauce,
> reflejando celestes armonías,
> y ahora que he dejado de sentirme
> soledad rumorosa, verde estela
> de ramas desplegadas al silencio,
> Señor, te lo suplico:
> hazme mujer aquí, para que pueda
> amar en alma y verso este paisaje.

(Sanz 1991: 17)

As in the first comparison with Atencia's poem, we see in 'Ordesa' an outline
of the distance covered, with the last transformation yet to take place, as in a

---

12.   Complete union with nature and sense of continuity are often present in her amorous
poems, even in a book like *Jardín de Murillo*, which she has designated as descriptive: 'Hoy sé
que el azahar que vela y duerme | sigue abriéndose al fondo de mi alma (Sanz 1991b: 41). The
following lines of Quevedo selected as epigraph for *Contemplaciones* underscore it: 'Basta ver
una vez grande hermosura, | que una vez vista eternamente enciende' (Sanz 1988: 9).

poem from *Trasluz* that ends with 'sólo queda partir a lo más hondo' (1991b: 157). This is very much in line with Bachelard's specification (1971: 51, 54): 'La dialectique du masculin et du féminin se déroule sur un rythme de la profondeur. Elle va du moins profond, toujours moins profond (le masculin) au toujours plus profond, toujours plus profond (le féminin)... En cette profondeur indéterminée règne le repos féminin.' That which in 'Ordesa' is formulated as a supplication has become reality in one of the most telling examples of Atencia's consummate art, which embodies a woman's vision:

LAGUNA DE FUENTEPIEDRA

Llegué cuando una luz muriente declinaba.
Emprendieron el vuelo los flamencos dejando
el lugar en su roja belleza insostenible.
Luego expuse mi cuerpo al aire. Descendía
hasta la orilla un suelo de dragones dormidos
entre plantas que crecen por mi recuerdo sólo.

Levanté con los dedos el cristal de las aguas,
contemplé su silencio y me adentré en mí misma.

(Atencia 1990: 244)

BIRUTÉ CIPLIJAUSKAITÉ

University of Wisconsin

THE ANXIETY OF CONFLUENCE:
JAMES JOYCE'S 'THE DEAD' AND
CLARICE LISPECTOR'S 'A PARTIDA DO TREM'

JAMES JOYCE'S story 'The Dead' describes the experience of a middle-aged
Dublin academic, Gabriel Conroy, at an annual Christmas party hosted by his
aunts, the Misses Morkan. Against a background of traditional seasonal rituals –dinner, musical recital, dancing, and speeches– the story traces the
gradual decline of Gabriel's self-confident public persona. All his conver-
sational initiatives with female friends and relations are in one way or another
rebuffed or frustrated. Even his after-dinner speech feels artificial and pre-
tentious. Finally, he takes a coach home from the party through the snow to
the Gresham Hotel where he is staying with his wife, Gretta. His growing
feelings of desire for his wife are thwarted when she begins to cry. The
singing at the party of an old Irish song, *The Lass of Aughrim*, has made her
recall the sad story of a former lover, Michael Furey, who, in her distant
youth, braved a freezing Galway winter for love of her, only to die of expo-
sure. As Gretta falls asleep, Gabriel's subjective disintegration is complete,
and he finally accepts the mortality of all humanity evoked in the figure of the
snow 'falling faintly through the universe and faintly falling, like the descent of
their last end, upon all the living and the dead' (242).[1]

Clarice Lispector's 'A partida do trem' narrates the thoughts and feelings
of two passengers who find themselves sharing a compartment on an early-
morning railway journey in present-day Brazil. The older of the two women,
Dona Maria Rita, is leaving the house of an uncaring daughter to go and live
with her son. The younger woman, Angela Pralini, is leaving her repressive

---

1. Textual quotations are from Lispector (1980) and Joyce (1993). The story of Gretta and
Michael Furey was closely based on an episode in Joyce own life, as Ellmann has shown (1959:
252–63).

academic lover Eduardo, in order to go and stay with her aunt and uncle in
the country. Little real dialogue is exchanged and yet an unspoken emotional
bond develops between the two women – the one close to death, the other
fearful of dying. The bond is further underlined by the fact that Dona Maria
Rita feels rejected by her daughter and Angela Pralini has no parents. Both
women become aware of their limitations as they observe each other and
imagine each other's thoughts. When Angela's journey ends she leaves Dona
Maria Rita asleep on the train. She tries to imagine the older woman's surprise when, on waking up, she will discover that Angela has vanished.

*   *   *   *   *

STARTING FROM a post-Lacanian French feminist position, this study will con-
sist of a comparative reading of 'A partida do trem' and 'The Dead' and will
examine the specific role played by dialogue in the two stories to construct
gendered subjectivities. I will use Lispector to open a classic Joyce text to
possible feminist readings, consciously reversing orthodox, patriarchal literary
history which would see Joyce as an influence on Lispector.[2] Indeed, 'A partida do trem' deliberately explodes any connotations of 'influence' through the
metafictional inclusion of overt textual references: Lispector's heroine, Angela, gives up reading Joyce 'porque ele era chato' (41) and prefers the company of her dog, Ulysses, who, she hastens to add 'não tem nada a ver com
Ulisses de Joyce'.

My purpose here is to follow up Hélène Cixous's claim (1992: 9) that 'on
two different sides of sexual difference' Portrait of the Artist and Perto de
Coração Selvagem 'stage the same scene'.[3] Focusing on dialogue, I shall dis-

---

2.   The similarity between the short stories of Joyce and those of Lispector has long been
recognized.   According to Earl Fitz, Lispector's mentor and fellow writer Lúcio Cardoso
'suggested that Lispector take the title of her first manuscript [Perto do Coração Selvagem] from
a line in Joyce's A Portrait of the Artist as a Young Man' (Fitz 1985: 6). Fitz identifies the stylistic overlap in their revolutionary short-story techniques: 'These [thematic and stylistic] interests, always rooted in Lispector's fascination with language and with the mystery and power of
the human mind, help show how much her stories have in common with Joyce's stories, especially those of Dubliners (1916)' (Fitz 1985: 97).

3.   Cixous's various 'readings with' Lispector have been increasingly – and in some respects
justifiably – criticized for 'writing as' Lispector in what amounts to intertextual appropriation.
In 'Hélène Cixous and the Hour of Clarice Lispector', Anna Klobucka takes a particularly
strong line against what she calls the 'belle love-affaire' and the erosion of Lispector's texts in a
semiotic interplay of the kind favoured by a French feminist 'industry' which lacks knowledge of

cuss how, 'on two different sides of sexual difference', 'The Dead' and 'A partida do trem' also effectively 'stage the same scene'.

In the two stories, exchanges of dialogue correlate to different states of mind. The balance between interior monologue and 'exterior' dialogue is used to mark a shift toward expression of the body, a voicing of the unconscious, and a recognition of mortality. Where Joyce's hero, Gabriel, increasingly opposes the fiction of an identity based on woman as a negative counterpart to man, Lispector's heroine, Angela, fictionalizes this opposition as a pretextual assumption. Both stories engage in a poetic deconstruction of male domination to expose the unstable, inherently fictional nature of subjectivity as we find it in the theories of Lacan. 'A partida do trem' starts from the subjective disintegration with which 'The Dead' concludes.[4] I shall first offer a brief account of the principles of Lacanian and French feminist theory which underpin my reading, and then review specific examples of how subjectivity relates to dialogue in both texts, and how multiple sensuality, evoked through écriture féminine, corresponds to a rejection of 'external' dialogue in favour of interior monologue. Finally, I shall examine how this heightened sensuality corresponds, in its turn, to a growing awareness of physical mortality and a potentially regenerative acceptance of death.

*   *   *   *   *

MY READING presupposes a Lacanian vision, as summarized by Leonard:

> 'The Woman' is a symptom which the man believes in in order to keep at bay the fragmentary, non-identificatory, pre-mirror (sic) phase that permanently undermines his subjective consciousness... 'The Woman' is a symptom. She exists, like Tinkerbell, because a man believes in her.
>
> (Leonard 1991: 459)

and sensitivity to the original Portuguese. While Klobucka offers a timely warning, her remarks refer mainly either to Cixous's dialogues with Lispector's texts or to the proliferation of inaccuracy and misunderstanding among Cixous's circle of acolytes. Klobucka does not engage with, for example, the early cornerstones of Cixous's post-Lacanian stance in *La jeune née* or *Le sexe ou la tête*. The progressive concepts first articulated in these books remain, I believe, a fruitful avenue of feminist enquiry.

4.   Margot Norris (1994: 192) takes a typically French feminist line as she explains: 'Highly experimental writing... which proclaims itself as having nothing significant to tell the reader, acts out, in the view of French feminism, a set of values (antidogmatism, decidability (sic), playfulness) that can be designated as feminine writing (*écriture féminine*) in distinction to patriarchal writing that arrogates truth, knowledge, and authority to itself.'

Cixous's theories of *écriture féminine* constitute a radical departure from Lacan's view of woman as a symptom whose purpose is to mask, no matter how
ineffectually, the 'split subjectivity' of masculine identity.[5] Nelly Furman explains the importance for Cixous's position of the Lacanian relationship between 'entry into language' and the 'split within the subject':

> The primitive union with the mother is ruptured at the mirror stage,
> which is the moment when the child recognizes its reflected image, identi-
> fies with it, and becomes aware of being a separate entity from the
> mother. The moment at which the infant perceives itself as an image, as
> 'other', is also the moment when the 'I' which does the perceiving is split
> off from the 'I' which is perceived. Seeing oneself as other determines an
> everlasting frustration and vain attempts at making one's 'I' and one's
> imago coincide, as well as a desire for oneness under the guise of other-
> ness... The mirror stage is the initial step in the process of an individual's
> integration in the social system; it marks the child's entrance into the
> symbolic order which is the realm of what Lacan calls the Law-of-the-Fa-
> ther or Name-of-the-Father.[6]

(1985: 70 – 71)

Cixous takes issue with Lacan because male sexual identity is formulated
when the girl is perceived as an absence, as a defective other, thus leaving the
field clear for the phallus to act as transcendental signifier in the construction
of language. To do this, she introduces the concept of bisexual writing, which
assumes the presence of, or at least an openness to, the possibility of both
sexes. However, she claims (1975: 85) that:

> For historical reasons at the present time it is woman who benefits from
> and opens up within this bisexuality beside itself (*sic*), which does not
> annihilate differences but cheers them on, pursues them, adds more: in a

---

5.   Leonard (1991: 459) cites the following from the introduction to Rose & Mitchell (1982):
'Lacan's point ... is not that women do not exist but that her status as an absolute category and
guarantor of fantasy ... is false ... Woman is the place on to which lack (*sic*) is projected and
through which it is simultaneously disavowed – woman is a "symptom" for the man.'

6.   Leonard's analysis of the 'The Dead' refers throughout to the split subject using Lacan's
terms – the *je* and the *moi*: 'The speaking subject he calls *je* or "I". The object-like stable
sense of subjectivity, what we might call an ideal sense of our identity, Lacan designates as the
moi or "me".' (Leonard 1991: 451).

certain way woman is bisexual – man having been trained to aim for glorious phallic monosexuality.[7]

Certain figures of speech are taken to be more useful than others for expressing the historically repressed female unconscious in Cixous's potentially 'bisexual' *écriture feminine*. Ann Rosalind Jones, for example, characterizes the practice of *écriture feminine* in terms (1985: 88) of 'double or multiple voices, broken syntax, repetitive or cumulative rather than linear structure, open endings'. As will become evident, this suggests sensuality and the primacy of touch, smell, and sound over sight. As Cixous indicates, 'There is tactility in the feminine text, there is touch, and this touch passes through the ear' (1981: 54).

*　　*　　*　　*　　*

RETURNING TO the interplay of self/other seen through close reading of dialogue, there is an overlap between Gabriel's enforced retreat into interior monologue in 'The Dead' and Angela's conscious selection of interior monologue in 'A partida do trem'. Unsuccessful attempts at public dialogue with women at the party drive Gabriel deeper into third-person or 'indirect' interior monologue, a common device in stream-of-consciousness narratives and one indicated by the adoption of free indirect style.[8] A clear example occurs when, in order to draw negative inferences about Gabriel's nationalist loyalties, Molly Ivors pounces on the paper to which he has contributed:

> A look of perplexity appeared on Gabriel's face. It was true that he wrote a literary column every Wednesday in *The Daily Express* for which he was paid fifteen shillings. But that did not make him a West Briton, surely.

(204)

7.　According to Toril Moi (1985: 99): 'The speaking subject that says "I am" is in fact saying "I am he (she) who has lost something" – and the loss suffered is the loss of the imaginary identity with the mother and with the world. The sentence, "I am" can best be translated as "I am that which I am not" according to Lacan. This re-writing emphasizes the fact that the speaking subject only comes into existence because of the repression of the desire for the lost mother. To speak as a subject is therefore to represent the existence of repressed desire: the speaking subject *is* lack (*sic*).'

8.　Free indirect style can be characterized as a manner of presenting the thoughts or utterances of a fictional character as if from that character's point of view by combining grammatical and other features of the character's direct speech with elements of the narrator's 'indirect' reporting style.

Lispector's female characters in 'A partida do trem' engage almost exclusively in a combination of first-person and indirect interior monologue. However, for Angela Pralini, interior monologue also gives way to snatches of implied dialogue with an absent other, her lover Eduardo, whom she is in the process of leaving for good. Thus, in addition to the two types of monologue already referred to, Lispector employs a third device to denote inner reflection in the form of interior dialogue, also indicated by free direct style.[9] The following example shows indirect interior monologue framed by two examples of interior dialogue:

> Segura minha mão Eduardo, para eu não ter medo de morrer. Mas ele não segurava nada. Só fazia era: pensar, pensar e pensar. Ah, Eduardo quero a doçura de Schumann.

> (32)

The exchanges of dialogue which mark the construction of subjectivity in 'The Dead' are also present in 'A partida do trem', but here, by being used together with different types of interior monologue, they are transformed into a reflective, imaginary process broadly suggestive of the language of psychotherapy.

I will now briefly discuss the dialogue/monologue relationship in 'The Dead' before moving to draw comparisons with 'A partida do trem'. In 'The Dead', Gabriel Conroy is frustrated in his attempts to make the women he encounters at the Christmas party respond to him in the way he expects and requires. External dialogue is implicitly negated. Neither Molly nor Lily greets his verbal overtures in a way that might help sustain his 'subjective unity', and Gabriel is obliged to take refuge in introspection. The women refuse to help him to continue to treat the 'subjective split of masculine identity' as if it did not exist. A series of unconnected exchanges at the social gathering show the reciprocal shattering of 'mirrored' identities. The first of these occurs between Lily and Gabriel, who makes a fool of himself on his arrival by making false assumptions about Lily's age and her interest in men. According to Leonard (1991: 456), Joyce shows Lily being created as a fictional self by imagining herself the way the other is likely to perceive her:

> We can guess that, on a strictly physical level, Lily is tired. But in order to give this feeling 'meaning' and identify it as her own, she must imbue it

---

9.   Free direct style has been described as a style 'shorn of conventional orthographical clues', such as punctuation, and is often used for first-person interior monologue.

with a subjective dimension by transforming it into language that she imagines could be spoken about her.

Lily cuts dead Gabriel's attempt to treat her as a child when he asks if she is going to get married. She replies, 'The men that is now is only palaver and what they can get out of you' (193). As Leonard points out (1991: 458), in this exchange each has been shattered as a mirror for the other but, 'Unwittingly, he shattered for her first by asking a real woman a question better asked about a little girl in a fairy-tale (of course, she is that unreal to him).' The shattering point between Lily and Gabriel occurs precisely when Lily's image of herself meets Gabriel's overmastering desire to keep his conscious subjectivity intact, when he requires her to respond to his question as if she were something which she is not. As Leonard (1991: 451) reminds us:

> The successful seduction of the other, through speech, permits the subject to authenticate his own subjectivity because, for the length of time that he is speaking, his belief that the audience believes in him allows him to believe in himself.

This is most obviously manifested in 'The Dead' through Gabriel's recurrent angst about the content of his after-dinner speech.

Turning now to the construction of dialogue in 'A partida do trem', we see that, where Gabriel interacts with others in a social, public context, the two female figures in 'A partida do trem' interact, for the most part, at the level of the subconscious. The protagonists – the seventy-seven year-old, Dona Maria Rita, and the thirty-seven year-old, Angela Pralini – are sitting opposite each other on the train. Only one male character speaks in Lispector's story and he performs a particular role, as we shall see. Men are otherwise absent. The words of men are implied in their absence and by their absence, as when Angela incorporates into her inner monologue her own spoken initiatives in an imagined dialogue with Eduardo. This recalls a well-known technique in Gestalt therapy: arguing with an empty chair. Angela is thus mentally re-writing the dialogues which have previously 'written her'.

Only one instance of 'mirror shattering', analogous to those which characterize 'The Dead', is demonstrated in 'A partida do trem'. This occurs when a male/female exchange is voiced in public. The only male to address either woman is the polite boy passenger who plays music on his transistor and offers to close the window. By addressing Maria Rita as 'A senhora' he restores her sense of composure. (Lispector characteristically employs a double negative to describe this as a loss of lack of composure.) The sudden male intervention frightens Maria Rita out of all normal proportion: 'Ah! exclamou ela, aterrorizada' (23). Angela resents the boy for disturbing her silent observation of Dona Maria Rita: 'Oh não!, pensou Angela, estava-se estragando tudo, o rapaz não deveria ter dito isso, era demais, não se devia tocá-la de novo'. The boy's subjectivity requires that Maria Rita should need things to be done for her. Echoing Leonard's view that Gabriel treats Lily like a little girl in a fairytale, the boy treats Dona Maria Rita like a helpless little old lady. For Maria Rita, as for Lily the maid, some form of authority, however illusory, must be asserted in response: 'Não, não, não, disse ela com falsa autoridade, de modo algum obrigado, só queria olhar'. Feeling herself suddenly observed by the boy, Maria Rita performs inauthentically: she hastily assumes the mask of the woman, as man's 'symptom' and, significantly, is immediately connected to the visual world – 'só queria olhar'. As Cixous puts it (1992: 9):

> The more one is elevated intellectually, the less one smells, the more one sees farther and farther. One enters into an intellectual dimension. Hearing is much closer to the body, to the ear.

*   *   *   *   *

HAVING OUTLINED the investment which masculine subjectivity has in dialogue in both texts, I shall now suggest how interior monologue and subjective disintegration correspond to syntactical fragmentation and the evocation of sensuality with a particular emphasis on sound and speech. Lispector's textual appeal to the senses requires the reader to pay more attention to the oral quality of language than to the visual act of reading. Bearing in mind Cixous's statement that 'There is tactility in the feminine text, there is touch, and this touch passes through the ear', we can see that her story periodically becomes rhythmic and musical. Angela uses onomatopoeia to calm her terror of death and the void. She longs for the comfort of Schumann's music and tells herself a childish story about a man walking on a vast carpet of smooth, shining fruit, making a beautiful sound underfoot. This repeated image binds the senses of hearing and touch into one simultaneous experience (37):

> Era tal a abundância de jabuticabas que ele se dava ao luxo de pisá-las. E elas faziam um barulho muito gostoso. Faziam assim: cloc-cloc-cloc...

Angela recalls sounds and senses in the privacy of interior monologue as she systematically dismantles Eduardo's image of her physical body. She takes repossession of her own body in terms of its fragmented, separate elements: lips, breasts, nose, fingertips, eyes and eyelashes, teeth, ears, hands, and feet. In 'The Dead', in contrast, Gabriel's body fails to make its promised entrance through union with Gretta. His body only reasserts itself in the slow swooning of the soul as his subjective disintegration finally penetrates his previous denial of physical mortality.

As Cixous claims in her *L'Exil de James Joyce* (1972: 613), 'The Dead' turns on 'a single epiphany of multiple meaning (death in life, life in death, the presence of death, evocation of the dead, all the forms a mind could invent for the imagining of death or as a means of avoiding the notion)'. In specific terms, both stories give poetic primacy to sound and music and conspicuously evade logocentricity, which Cixous (1992: 9) equates with 'the intellectual dimension'. For Angela and Gabriel, psychic regeneration is ultimately effected through a prefiguration of mortality in the projected death of another.

Gabriel, like Angela, prefigures a death in his mind as he retraces the steps of the evening that caused him to feel so passionately towards his wife:

> Poor Aunt Julia! She too, would soon be a shade with the shade of Patrick Morkan and his horse. He had caught that haggard look upon her face for a moment when she was singing *Arrayed for the Bridal*.
>
> (241)

For Gretta, too, the harbinger of death is a song, *The Lass of Aughrim*, which Bartell D'Arcy sings at the end of the party and which reminds her of Michael Furey, who used to sing it. Her tale of Michael Furey's death for love, told at the point where Gabriel is about to make love to his wife, forces him to learn, as Leonard puts it (1991: 467), 'suddenly and beyond any ability of his to equivocate, that Gretta will not authenticate that "something" in his voice that connects him to his belief in the woman and his own phallic function'. Thus, Gabriel is figuratively alienated from this own image in the hotel-room mirror when Gretta ceases to reflect for him. He contemplates himself at a distance as if he were separated from his own face:

> As he passed in front of the cheval-glass he caught sight of himself in full length, his broad, well-filled shirt-front, the face whose expression always puzzled him when he saw it in a mirror.
>
> (236)

Similarly, when Angela looks into her handbag mirror, her split subjectivity is indicated by the alternation of 'Angela' between subject and object pronoun positions. This makes her simultaneously the addresser and addressee of the same interior dialogue as she says to herself: 'Pareço-me com um desmaio. Cuidado com o abismo, digo àquela que se parece com um desmaio' (32). The 'desmaio' evokes both a loss of the senses in swooning, and a loss of meaning or sense, both of which are contained in the wordplay on 'perder (os) sentido(s)'. At the end of 'The Dead', Gabriel's subjective disintegration is conveyed in terms of a swoon:

> His soul swooned softly as he heard the snow falling faintly through the universe and faintly falling, like the descent of their last end, upon all the living and the dead.[10]

(242)

The life/death pairing in both texts is discernible through shifting states of consciousness and dissolution of limits. In a deconstructionist reading of 'The Dead', John Paul Riquelme suggests that Gabriel denies death by refusing to accept his human limitations and requiring that everything around him conform to his desires: 'He [Gabriel] ignores his own limits and, in effect, denies his own mortality... His desire for control is clear in the series of encounters with Lily, Miss Ivors, and Gretta' (Riquelme 1994: 229). Lispector's Dona Maria Rita also has to accept that death will not coincide with any of her desires and expectations but rather will overturn and surprise them: 'Como dona Maria Rita sempre fora uma pessoa comum, achava que morrer não era coisa normal. Morrer era surpreendente. Era como se ela não estivesse à altura do ato de morte...' (30). In *L'Exil*, Cixous's reading of the conclusion to 'The Dead' focuses similarly on a dissolution of limits as she writes:

> To the accompaniment of a verbal music, the soul that had perceived its outward appearance in the mirror is dissolved in that one and only phase of time when the boundaries of life and death are buried under the snow, swooning into sleep.

(1972: 615)

10.   Sheldon Brivic's Lacanian reading of 'The Dead', interestingly illuminates Gretta's loss as a catalyst for Gabriel's disintegration and its expression in terms of soul. He suggests (1991: 180) that 'The loss the woman thinks of expresses the depth of her subjectivity, drawing back veils as no other feeling could in accord with Lacan's principle that the subject is built on a sense of loss. Perhaps it is because identity springs from separation that only by seeing the woman's loss can the artist see his own soul'.

Both texts end with sleep, or more precisely, with a wakeful figure observing a sleeper. Angela's final image is of a sleeping Dona Maria Rita: 'Ficou-a perturbando a visão da velha quando acordasse, a imagem do seu rosto espantado diante do banco vazio de Angela' (43). Gabriel also observes Gretta fast asleep: 'The thought of how she who lay beside him had locked in her heart for so many years that image of her lover's eyes...' (241). Referring to these closing images of 'The Dead', Cixous writes:

> Joyce here has contrived not only to detach the images from their spatial context but also to develop two parallel movements of images against a temporal background... [with the effect that] art no longer consists simply of reproducing vision or dialogue, but itself generates visions.
>
> (1972: 615)

The closing scene of 'A partida do trem' generates the future vision of Dona Rita, waking up to find Angela's seat empty, after she has left the train. Thus, an intimate, localized image of projected absence corresponds to Gabriel's cosmic projection of Michael Furey's mortality on the whole of humanity including himself. The concluding lines of both texts give rise to visions of the future, carried beyond the closing lines of the stories by the drifting snow and the moving train. They are of a future of absence and loss, and serve to remind readers of their own mortality.

HILARY OWEN

University of Manchester

WHATEVER HAPPENED TO BABY BOYS?:
MOTHERHOOD AND DEATH
IN LYDIA FAGUNDES TELLES

IN PORTUGUESE WE HAVE A SAYING: 'Mães há só uma', which translates as 'You only have one mother'. Like much received wisdom, this particular nugget elicits a multiplicity of reactions. Firstly, it may be true that there is only ever one mother, but, as I shall argue, a mother can be many things. Secondly, if some of these things are, in real life, anything like the stuff of which the average mother in the works of Lygia Fagundes Telles is made, one must be thankful for small mercies. In the narrative fiction of Fagundes Telles – both her short stories and her novels – the figure of the mother appears both as multi-faceted and uniformly dangerous.

Fagundes Telles's work achieved an early and lasting success both in Brazil and abroad. This is, perhaps, surprising considering her determination to trespass upon a series of conventions which lie at the heart of Brazilian cultural identity. This study will focus on her narrative treatment of the theme of maternity and will argue that it underpins a stance which, whether regarded from the specific perspective of gender or viewed in the wider context of social politics, is consistently transgressive.

Maternity as an event intrinsic to womanhood (an old and old-fashioned conviction, both in a Brazilian social context and in the Western Judaeo-Christian tradition) is radically revised by Fagundes Telles in a highly idiosyncratic rendering of the mothering phenomenon. Her female protagonists, almost without exception, compound their kinship bonds and social ties as the sisters, daughters, wives, lovers, and cousins of men with the added dimension of a motherliness which is as pernicious –for men– as was the disobedient action of the first mother in Genesis for mankind.

June Hahner has referred to Brazil (1990: xii) as a 'country without a memory', a problem she links to the difficulties faced by historians who seek to document a variety of phenomena in Brazilian history and, specifically, in women-oriented historiography. Yet what emerges from her detailed account of the struggle for women's rights in the period between 1850 and the 1980s is an obsession with the figure of the mother as the origin and creator of both self and nation. In any attempt to understand the gender struggle in Brazil over the last century, the mother becomes a crucial icon, invoked either by those who point to her traditional role as the guardian and guarantor of the *status quo*, or by those who, while paying lip-service to conventional views of the institution of motherhood, invoke her importance as first educator of children and as a justification for the expansion of all women's rights to equality in education, employment, marriage, and every other aspect of the law (Hahner 1990: 42–96).

At the core of this battle of conflicting ideologies and aims, the figure of the mother becomes shrouded in a confusion of contradictory needs and desires that consistently cast her as the figure who most directly furthers the particular interests promoted. The mother is both all-powerful in the home and infinitely manipulable; she is omnipotent and powerless, adored and hated, a permanent point of reference and an outcast. She is always dangerous.

The ambivalence about the role of the mother, reflected in Brazilian law by remnants of the Philippine Code (which perpetuated a woman's legal dependence upon her husband's authority for purposes of employment, inheritance, property, pension, travel, and the possession of a bank account) was one factor among many that acted as constraints on the development of a Brazilian women's movement until the later decades of this century. Throughout the 1970s and 1980s, for example, fear of offending even the more progressive faction within the Catholic Church hindered the feminist lobby, in which Fagundes Telles has been a self-declared activist (Telles 1983: 11–14), when it attempted to address radical issues such as birth control, abortion, the concept of a woman's exclusive rights over her own body, and an understanding of the role of the mother (Hahner 1990: 197–204).

The female body that gives birth to life has never ceased to be a mystery. This perplexity is not confined to Brazil but is generally prevalent in the Western psyche. The scars that have resulted from attempts to claim or reclaim the female body constitute the very texture of the writing of authors such as Fagundes Telles. Like her, however, both in Brazil and beyond, the innumerable fictional and non-fictional voices in literature, theory, sociology, history, psychiatry, and medicine have understood the process of motherhood as encompassing both the moment of origin of a *status quo* and the moment when it first becomes possible to imagine the obliteration of the *status quo*.

In one of his essays in *Literature and Evil*, Georges Bataille argues, possibly anti-intuitively but none the less persuasively, that sexuality and reproduction, entailing the reproduction of the single into the multiple, the giving of one's body to the making of another or others, foreshadow not immortality but death, the loss of the unique self (1985: 13–31). God may succeed in being both single and infinite, but the transition from one to many, or from one to infinity, in the realm of the human is, according to Franz Endres, the move away from innocence to perdition, from unity with the singleness of the God-head and immortality to excommunication and dissolution (1993: 13–14). Never more so, possibly, than in the multiplication act inherent in mothering.

Here is a conundrum. A gun holds six bullets. Playing Russian roulette with one bullet in the chamber offers a one-in-six possibility of dying. Estimates vary widely but, until antibiotics to combat infection became generally available in the second half of this century, it would seem that as many as one woman in every three or four died in childbirth.[1] Sometimes the figures were even more alarming: according to one source, for example, 'in the French province of Lombardy in one year no single woman survived childbirth' (Rich 1992: 151; Flandrin 1979: 217–21). It follows that historically, until as recently as fifty years ago, it was often safer to play Russian roulette than to be a sexually active woman of child-bearing age.

The implications of this for family dynamics are not negligible. Prior to the advent of regular medical hygiene, contraceptives, and antibiotics, every time a woman had sex she was faced with the prospect of pregnancy or even of death. One woman in every three or four gestated inside her own body her potential murderer; one man in every three or four lived out the larger part of his adulthood aware that he had exacted pleasure at the price of another's death. One person in every three or four lived an entire existence in the awareness of having attained life at the price of that of another, the mother. For a girl, atonement for involuntary matricide might lie in the subsequent surrender of life, in her turn, to the reproductive imperative, often patriarchal and patrilinear. For a boy, involuntary matricide became an additional factor

---

1. Figures supplied by Flandrin (1979) suggest a figure closer to one in ten, but point to huge variations and to problems of interpretation.

in that complex agglomeration of psychic phenomena which some have seen as the male dread and guilt of being of woman born.

In this century, an understanding of family dynamics cannot ignore the Freudian formula which takes as one of its hypotheses the Oedipal discarding by both sexes of the mother and the identification (albeit, in the late-Freudian view, an acknowledgedly asymmetrical identification) of each sex with the father.[2] According to Lacan, the loss or relinquishing of the mother is a prerequisite to entry into the Symbolic: an entry which signals the acceptance (or repression) of the loss of that mother and of a state before self, before identity. This enables the concomitant assimilation of a concept of self, language, culture, community, and society, which constitute the 'Order of the Symbolic'. Starting with the ideas of Freud, and to a lesser extent of Lacan, Nancy Chodorow (1979), Dorothy Dinnerstein (1987), and other psychoanalytic revisionists see as central to both the conflict and the final identification with the father a much more fundamental and instinctive need to escape from the mother, who represents a threat not just to freedom but to the very integrity of the self. Psychically, according to Dinnerstein, the dominion of the father will become apparent as a less ominous alternative and therefore as preferable to the fundamental danger embodied by the mother. Post-Freudian feminist revisionism accordingly begins where mainstream Freudian thought, having hinted at the mother as the real source of psychic menace, abandons her to concentrate on the figure of the father. Revisionist psychoanalytic feminist thought works backward from this to reinstate the maternal as the focus of its analysis.

Chodorow, Dinnerstein, and Patricia Waugh (1989) variously describe how, in a culture in which the care of children falls almost exclusively to women, the mother is at one and the same time the first love, the first witness, and the first source of frustration for the child. The mother holds absolute power of life or death over the infant, a fact which lies not only at the heart of the nature of relations between the sexes in adulthood, but also underpins certain contradictions inherent in the subsequent knowledge that the supposedly all-powerful mother is, after all, disempowered in a patriarchal society.

Be that as it may, the mother – omnipotent mediator between the infant and all that is external to him or her – is the source of all that the newborn

---

2.   The framework first developed in *Three Essays on Sexuality* was subsequently revised throughout the post-1925 writings (Freud 1961a, 1961b, 1984).

child experiences as good and also all that is experienced as bad. Her power gradually becomes comprehensible both as the gift of life and as the embodiment of the terror of *finite* life, or death. The awareness of this dual effect will persist in post-infancy stages through into adult consciousness as both the desire for and the dread of a return to the Nirvana-like womb which promises both binding pleasure and boundless dissolution. The mother herself, the site of that dangerous womb, also triggers the knowledge of the finiteness of life and the inevitability of death for all those for whom she also represents the only possible beginning. As such, she represents an assault against a masculine identity informed by the recognition of the originating body of that mother and the knowledge of its own mortality. When the possessors of that male identity are the nation's sons, the mother may become the purveyor of cultural annihilation.

*   *   *   *   *

AGAINST THIS BACKGROUND of phantasmic and fantastic motherhood I shall seek to arrive at an understanding of the narrative fiction of Fagundes Telles, troubled as it is by an obsession with figures of mothers who go about their mothering with malice aforethought. An insight into the murderous nature of motherhood in Telles's work, moreover, extends further into what amounts to a gender agenda operating through desecration. Almost every one of her female protagonists, in one way or another, through symbolic (but more often real) murder – real although sometimes muted by devices of allegory, horror, or the fantastic – commits a crime which has threefold implications. Murder itself (which is, by definition, transgressive) is compounded by gender aggression (the female invariably murdering the male). It is further aggravated by an internecine dimension, since the murderesses of husbands and lovers are always, after a fashion, also the metaphorical mothers of these men – men invariably infantilized and emasculated by a variety of means, abducted from the 'Symbolic Order', and returned to a non-speaking, regressive, or infantile dependency which proves lethal.

Similarly, the infantilization of the male prior to his annihilation is paralleled by the subsuming of the various roles previously held by female protagonists into the overriding one of the mother. But this is a punitive, castrating

mother whose purpose it is to negate the male in his socially and metaphysi-
cally empowered capacities.

Male monotheisms attributing the power of creation to a paternal God underpin the aesthetic assumption of the begetting of artistic voice as akin to the
begetting of a son, and as an affirmation of sexual prowess and presence
linked to the possession of a male libido (Gilbert & Gubar 1984: 3–44). The
usurping by men of the procreative monopoly has arguably had a bearing
upon the oscillations of gender power ever since female-centered cosmologies
were toppled by 'male' monotheisms (Miles 1989: 36–102; Kristeva 1993:
139–45). In the aftermath of the rise of God the Father and God the Son, the
rise of the phallus over the womb, women speak on sufferance and when they
do so it is as an act of transgression against a standing injunction to silence, a
transgression which turns them into what one critic terms 'thieves of language'
(Ostriker 1986: 314). They cannibalize an order which has never willingly
granted them membership. The demarcation of the limits of the confidence
trick ensures a male monopoly over voice and also over procreation. The
staking of the procreative territory as an inaugural act of hostility may offer
one way into understanding a writer such as Fagundes Telles and, with her, a
host of other women writers. Angela Carter, Fay Weldon, and Margaret
Atwood are all, in their different ways, spokeswomen for the act of writing as
a frightening, deliberate, thoughtful, programmatic loss of control.

In Fagundes Telles's work we face an onslaught against, among other targets, her readers, whom she denies the comfort of secure role identifications.
These, whether those of the victims or of the perpetrators, cannot be adopted
without unease. When the masks of deceptive acceptability are snatched away
from the mothers, wives, cousins, lovers, and *namoradas* of stories such as 'O
jardim selvagem' (1981: 47–56), 'A estrutura da bolha de sabóo' (1984a:
131–35), 'Apenas um saxofone' (1984a: 21–29), and 'Herbarium' (1984b:
41–49), the process Baudrillard (1988: 166–84) has described as the murder
of the real by its simulacrum, or the viral attack perpetrated against 'a modern
context' by a set of more 'archaic' terms – the speakers of the 'evil' which
modern orthodoxy can no longer voice (1993: 81–88) – is exhibited in its
definitive form. At the heart of this process, in the work of Fagundes Telles,
the figure of the mother always lurks as the site of the dangerous unspoken or
unconscious.

This return of the repressed is broached by Kristeva in *Powers of Horror* where she describes it as 'the site of the other' (1982: 54). What she terms 'abjection' is, in the Georges Bataille definition she draws upon, 'the inability to assume with sufficient strength the imperative act of excluding abject things', or otherness – an act which, if successful, 'establishes the foundations of collective existence' (1982: 56). She sees the prohibition of the abject, and the *attitude* of abjection (the Bataillian consciousness of the weakness of that prohibition, indicative of the frailty of the 'Symbolic Order') as the key to an understanding of the relationship with the mother (1982: 64 – 69). According to Kristeva, the real threshold that demarcates the clean from the unclean lies not between man and woman, nor between woman and son, but between woman as desiring/speaking being and woman as mother. If this is so, then the transgression of that necessary threshold (necessary if the Symbolic Order is to remain intact) –the abolition of the lawful demarcation that separates mothers from lovers– ushers in cultural annihilation. In the works of Fagundes Telles, the woman is not unconsciously, unavoidably, or blamelessly the incestuous mother/lover but is so *by choice.* She is driven to transform herself into a Jocasta figure by a transgressive imperative which becomes totally disruptive. She first mothers and then kills her emasculated, sickly, fragile child/husband or vulnerable father. So seditious is this act that, unsurprisingly, its ripples extend beyond the realm of gender and procreation into the spheres of orthodoxy, logic, realism, and science. In these stories, the immediate impact is on language and on the power of utterance. Because interference (in the form of incest or murder or both) with the expected cycles of reproduction, whether biological or social, is the most virulent of all possible insurrections, the hijacking and perversion of the maternal function becomes a taboo subject. It thus acquires an extra dimension of horror through the very insistence of the author on uttering it.

*   *   *   *   *

I SHALL CONCENTRATE here on an analysis of two short stories by Fagundes Telles which in different ways illustrate the tension between maternal love and maternal destruction of the son in secular and theological contexts respectively: 'Verde lagarto amarelo' (1984a: 11–20) and 'Natal na barca' (1986: 135–41). For the development of the maternal role, 'Verde lagarto amarelo'

depends on an identification between the figure of the mother, already dead
when the story begins, and that of her younger son, Eduardo, whose agency, as
I shall argue, is that of heir to both the maternal and paternal legacies – unlike his elder brother, Rodolfo, a man who is ill at ease and ultimately destroyed. As in so many of Fagundes Telles's short stories, the plot focuses on
an atmosphere which, even when it does not fulfil its potential for doing so,
none the less constantly threatens to slip into horror or the fantastic. The narrative focuses on a visit the Adonis-like, popular, married, father-to-be
younger brother, Eduardo, pays one stifling summer afternoon to the fat,
sweaty, morbid, semi-successful writer, Rodolfo, who lives alone in a apartment infested with cockroaches. On his arrival, Eduardo announces a surprise
to be disclosed at the end of the visit ('mostro depois', 1984a: 12), a surprise
whose potential for menace never diminishes during the course of the visit.
Eduardo is revealed, through Rodolfo's flashback and his own present actions,
to be a genuinely gentle, loving, considerate man and sibling who, none the
less, throughout their respective and shared pasts, has robbed Rodolfo of their
mother's love, a wife, a family, and popularity. The surprise revealed at the
end of the story is that Eduardo has written a novel and in doing so has finally
trespassed upon the last preserve left to his brother: authorship and voice.
The reader deduces from their past histories that Eduardo will outstrip
Rodolfo in this, too.

As we have suggested, Eduardo is both tender and destructive, and closely
associated with the mother's impact upon Rodolfo before her death. The
mother's love for her unpromising elder son was similarly ambivalent.
Eduardo's presence, therefore, as it impinges upon Rodolfo and all aspects of
his life, is both soothing and feral, as illustrated by his 'passo macio, sem
ruído, não chegava a ser felino: apenas um andar discreto. Polido'. In his
tender concern for his elder brother, however, Eduardo clearly controls the
power of gaze – 'nada lhe escapava' – through which he grasps the nature of
Rodolfo's vulnerabilities – 'ele sabe que sempre estou sozinho' (11) – and the
squalor of a life filled with cockroaches, chipped tea cups, sweaty glands, and
excess weight.

As was the case with the conditional nature of the mother's love for
Rodolfo – a love which, in a much less conditional form, Eduardo has taken it
upon himself to replace – the boundary between nurturing and destruction remains unstable. This is understood by Rodolfo, who describes himself as

having been, since childhood, 'condenado ao seu fraterno amor' (17). Thus, whether by claiming to have already had a cup of coffee in the street, and thereby shielding him from the humiliation of displaying his unwashed cups (12), or by persistently courting his company in the face of constant refusals, the love of the younger for the older brother never loses its aura of encircling, engulfing destructiveness which, to revert to psychoanalytic parlance, relegates Rodolfo to the helplessness of infancy, a helplessness which can be overcome only through moving away from the realm of maternal presence which, in the absence of the dead mother, lives on in the person of her younger son.

As the visit progresses and the tokens of Eduardo's brotherly love accumulate, they prove an overwhelming threat to Rodolfo. They prevent him from reaffirming his position as a fully integrated speaking and reproductive male within the Symbolic Order. Eduardo invites Rodolfo to be the godfather of his unborn son, an event which elicits in Rodolfo both the impetus to murder and the fear of death:

> – Para quando o filho?
> ...
> – No próximo mês, parece ... Não perdia um só dos meus movimentos. – E adivinha agora quem vai ser o padrinho.
> – Que padrinho?
> – Do meu filho, ora!
> – Não tenho a menor idéia.
> – Você.
> Minha mão tremia como se ao invés de açúcar eu estivesse mergulhando a colher em arsênico. Sentime infinitamente mais gordo. Mais vil. Tive vontade de vomitar.
> – Não faz sentido, Eduardo. Não acredito em Deus, não acredito em nada.
> – E daí? – perguntou ele, servindo-se de mais açúcar. Atraiu-me quase num abraço. – Fique tranquilo, eu acredito por nós dois.
> Tomei de um só trago o café amargo. Uma gota de suor pingou no pires. Passei a mão pelo queixo. Não pudera ser pai, seria padrinho.
>
> (16–17)

From Rodolfo's position, the role of godfather –*padrinho*, a diminutive form of the original *padre* or *pai*– assumes, as is habitual in his relations with his brother, a second-rate status. He is a father who is linguistically and in reality reduced to a 'little father', and therefore to a mock paternity which echoes Eduardo's prior theft of other emotional terrains.

Rodolfo's repeated fantasies of getting rid of Eduardo, either through distance – 'e se ele fosse morar longe' (17) – or, better still, by death, as signalled by his recollection of a childhood episode in which he experienced (and enjoyed) a premonition which was also a desire for Eduardo's death in a fight with another boy – 'vio ensanguentado, a roupa em tiras... Ouvi a voz da minha mãe chamando: "Rodolfo, Rodolfo!" Agora ela o carregava em prantos, tentando arrancar-lhe o canivete enterrado no peito até ao cabo' (19) – recall the Freudian suggestion that the childhood desire for the death of a sibling may be reactivated subsequently as the dream or fear of the death that was previously desired (Freud 1983: 347 – 74). Rodolfo's fantasies concerning Eduardo's death, which progress rapidly to a fear of his own destruction at the loving and retaliatory hands of his brother, re-enact the Freudian scenario of Oedipal fear of paternal retribution. In Rodolfo's case, however (and typically for Fagundes Telles, in whose work the power of the father is relegated to second place and surrenders to the superior menace of the maternal), the fantasies and the fear both refer back to the figure of the mother. Rodolfo also relives in detail the scene at his mother's deathbed and experiences yet again her rejection of him and the designation of Eduardo as her successor who will both love him and destroy him:

> Com os olhos cozidos de tanto chorar, ajoelhei-me e, fingindo arrumar-lhe o travesseiro, pousei a cabeça ao alcance da sua mão, ah, se me tocasse com um pouco de amor. Mas ela só via o broche, um caco de vidro que Eduardo achou no quintal e enrolou em fiozinhos de arame formando um casulo, 'mamãezinha querida, eu que fiz para você!' Ela beijou o broche. E o arame ficou sendo prata e o caco de garrafa ficou sendo esmeralda. Foi o broche que lhe fechou a gola do vestido. Quando me despedi, apertei sua mão gelada contra minha boca, e eu, mamãe, e eu?

(18)

If the Oedipal scenario differs here in having the mother as both the target of the son's murderous wish and the source of retaliation against that wish, the outcome of the Oedipal struggle will also differ in this story from the classical Freudian and post-Freudian resolution. The mother will not be successfully discarded by Rodolfo in favour of a transition to linguistically endowed masculinity, but will rather remain with him in perpetuity. Just as in childhood he relinquished the fantasy of Eduardo's death under the knife in the playground quarrel – 'mas ele não usou o canivete? perguntei' (19) – and carried him home on his back like a beast of burden – 'vamos, monta em mim' (19) – Rodolfo now accepts Eduardo's enduring presence in his life as a millstone around his neck: 'era tão magro, não era? Mas pesava como chumbo' (19). Simultaneously, he sees him as a vampire figure – 'vi nossa sombra no muro, as tiras [da camisa dele] se abrindo como asas' (19) – who will consume him and eventually deprive him of the essential trappings of fully integrated masculinity: sexuality, paternity, property – '[depois da morte de mamãe, até] os lençóis bordados, obriguei-o a aceitar tudo... Minha mãe. Depois, Ofélia. Porque não haveria de ficar também com os lençóis?' (15) – and, finally, creative language.

During Eduardo's visit, Rodolfo is forced into disturbing childhood reminiscences which trigger a return to the helplessness and chaos of that prelinguistic state against which, as a writer, he deploys the language he knows to be his last remaining preserve when faced with the onslaught of the maternal: 'era o que me restara: escrever' (20). But this is a preserve which Eduardo's presence and love deny, leaving him instead trapped in images of fragmentation and dispersal:

> Os ventos. Vazio. Imobilidade e vazio. Se eu ficar assim imóvel, respirando leve, sem ódio, sem amor, se eu ficar assim um instante, sem pensamento, sem corpo.
>
> (13)

Eduardo's theft of language and creativity at the end of the story, and its effect upon Rodolfo, once again remind us that Rodolfo has inherited the mission of his mother whose combination of concern and rejection acted in the past to destroy her elder son, through the lethal power of language:

> 'Esse menino transpira tanto, meus céus! Acaba de vestir roupa limpa e já começa a transpirar, nem parece que tomou banho. Tão desagradável!...' Minha mãe não usava a palavra suor que era forte demais para seu vocabulário, *ela gostava das belas palavras*, das belas imagens. Delicadamente falava em transpiração *com aquela elegância em vestir as palavras* como nos vestia... Era menino ainda mas houve um dia em que quis morrer para não transpirar mais.
>
> (14, emphasis added)

His brother's insistence on transporting Rodolfo back into childhood – 'na noite passada sonhei com a nossa antiga casa' (14) – which is also the realm of the maternal, imperils Rodolfo's fragile hold over language and masculinity. Thus Rodolfo's memory of a dream in which he is the Oedipal (and slim) son who is victorious over both father and mother and who dances with his mother to the accompaniment of a waltz played on the piano by his father, dissolves into the customary humiliation of an outbreak of sweating which alienates him again from that mother he dreams of conquering amorously and vanquishing existentially:

> Papai tocava piano e mamãe... Rodopiávamos vertiginosos numa valsa e eu era magro, tão magro que meus pés mal roçavam o chão, senti mesmo que levantavam vôo e eu ria, enlaçando-a em volta do lustre quando de repente o suor começou a escorrer, escorrer.
>
> (14)

The Oedipal wish is thus snatched from him at the moment of fulfilment and, if his reaction is the relinquishing of the mother and all that is connected with her in favour of his brother – 'o aparelho de chá, o faqueiro, os cristais e os tapetes tinham ficado com ele. Também os lençóis bordados, obriguei-o a aceitar tudo' (15) – the mother continues to pursue him beyond the grave in the person of her perfect son who, unlike Rodolfo, accomplishes the psycho-analytic feat of identifying with the father while retaining a foothold in the realm of the (dead) mother.

Eduardo, who inherits not only his mother's love and possessions but his father's masculinity and male accoutrements – 'fiquei a olhar as abotoaduras que tinham sido do meu pai' (13) – will finally steal from Rodolfo the prerogative of language and creativity which in adulthood the latter had carved out for himself in defiance of his linguistically gifted mother:

> Escritor, sim, mas nem aquele tipo de escritor de sucesso, convidado para festas, dando entrevistas na televisão: um escritor de cabeça baixa e calado, abrindo com as mãos em garra seu caminho.
>
> (17)

The mockery of decision-making about Eduardo's writing future, seemingly placed by Eduardo in Rodolfo's hands – 'você é quem vai decidir. Ponho nas suas mãos' (17) – does not in effect conceal the power Eduardo exercises over the situation. The surprise to be sprung upon Rodolfo in the last page, and heralded by the opening paragraphs – 'trouxe também uma coisa... Mostro depois' – contrasts even then with Rodolfo's wistfulness about a creative process whose demands he can only satisfy with difficulty: 'assim queria escrever, indo ao âmago até atingir a semente resguardada lá no fundo como um feto' (12).

Rodolfo understands all too clearly the profounder implications of the revelation of his brother's authorship. It signals the end of his own creative work, which, from now on, will be eclipsed and consigned to the obscurity symbolized by the drawer where he locks away his latest draft at the moment of the revelation:

> Tirei-lhe as folhas das mãos e fechei-as na gaveta. Era o que me restara: escrever. Será possível que ele também?... Olhei para sua pasta na cadeira e adivinhei a surpresa. Senti meu coração se fechar como uma concha. A dor era quase física. Olhei para ele. – Você escreveu um romance. É isso? Os originais estão na pasta... É isso?
> Ele então abriu a pasta.
>
> (20)

The use of the pluperfect tense, 'restara', signals the end of the dream of survival, and the introduction of an element of horror despite the surface uneventfulness of the plot. Having failed to kill his brother either in fact or in fantasy, Rodolfo must submit to having that brother lovingly and maternally kill him. Eduardo is Rodolfo's tender brother but also, and supremely, his mother's loving and his father's successful son. The consummate survivor, Eduardo progresses into the realm of language and into what Lacan has called the 'Law-of-the-Father', leaving behind him, as a dutiful compensatory gesture to the discarded dead mother, a sacrificial lamb, the re-infantilized body of his brother, now condemned to return to the maternal once again.

Post-Freudian theory has rescued the mother from the relegation to the pre-Oedipal stage to which she was consigned by Freud. In the fiction of Fagundes Telles, the incorporation of the limitations of the Freudian formula as well as of the revisions which an understanding of its dread of the maternal suggest, is also refracted through the prism of an older, underpinning Judaeo-Christian misogyny, as illustrated in the second story to be discussed here. In 'Natal na barca' (1986: 135–41), a first-person narrator, only belatedly disclosed as female, travels on a mysterious barge over an mysterious, purgatorial stretch of water, with a demonic Madonna figure who, holding her baby in her arms, mesmerizes the narrator with the tale of the death of her first child, and is encouraged in her murderous, story-telling, creative impulse. As fear escalates, the narrator realizes that the child in the arms of the story-teller is also dead. The catastrophe of the second death – death not birth – of this second Child on an improbably gory Christmas Eve, is not remedied by the eventual discovery by the narrator that she has made a mistake and that the second child in this uncannily rescripted Nativity is alive after all, albeit temporarily. The threat implicit in 'Natal na barca' is in the telling of what is, in the end, an anti-Nativity concern, a heretical Second Coming, in the course of which divine birth is metamorphosed into death everlasting:

> Ali estávamos os quatro, silenciosos como mortos num antigo barco de mortos deslizando na escuridão. Contudo, estávamos vivos. E era Natal.

> (135–36)

The scenario that emerges from the death narrative of the supposed *mater dolorosa* is not one of maternal regret or filial resuscitation or universal redemption. Rather, it is the portrait of an dead male line at war with the patriarchal Judaeo-Christian faith, and it results in the voicing by a woman and mother of the spectacle of a vanished God, his dead first-born Son and a dying second-born. The sons of God, already heretical for being not one and unique but two and replicable, threaten the original creed by proving to be mortal. The very declaration of faith on the part of this Virgin – 'a tal fé que removia montanhas' (139) – proves here to be earth-shattering in a different way, since the relocated mountains will rearrange the terrain upon which the voice will materialize and change gender. Thus, the mother's apparently conventional redemptive story of Christian resignation to her first child's death is threatened by the mistaken discovery (threatening while it lasts) on the part of her interlocutor that, while the story was being told by the mother, her second child has died in her arms. At the moment when the Kingdom of God appeared to have been reinstated on Earth through the agency of the female voice, that voice heralds instead the possibility of the death of a second child. The Virgin's last words to the narrator before she disappears into the night, 'então bom Natal!' (140), constitute the final denial of a set of fundamental premises, both religious and secular in character, and their replacement by a vacuum which is also the affirmation of an alternative (female) beginning.

Infanticide by the mother is an old nightmare. In the Talmud, Adam had a first wife, before Eve, named Lilith. Lilith refused God's injunction to submit to Adam and be his helpmate and, as a consequence of her mutiny, was banished to the edge of the Dead Sea, where she dwells to this day, in a cave, consorting with demons and devouring her male offspring in an insurrection against her husband and his Creator (Gilbert & Gubar 1984: 35; Kristeva 1993: 140). The second spouse hardly fared better: although Adam and Eve both underwent punishments as a consequence of the latter's misdemeanour, Eve and all her female successors suffered further punishments specific to the female archculprit, including menstruation, the pain of childbirth, and, arguably, breast-feeding – all of them sanctions attached to motherhood (Warner 1976: 204). The consequences of Eve's emergence as a reproductive, *knowing* woman following her theft of the fruit of the Tree of Knowledge, are seen to be so grave as to require an absolute reversal. Disempowerment is ensured by the subsequent rewriting of the theft of the apple as the 'Blessed Fall', theologically sanitized in the Virgin cult as the pretext for the cosmetic advent of Mary (mother of a Father's Son and herself the incubator of a Trinity), which pointedly excludes her as its third term and declares her to be more ghostly even than the preferred alternative of the archetypal Dove (Warner 1976). Thus a boys-only club is reinstated. The single, profoundly unacceptable role-model alternative to Mary's womanhood, at the opposite extreme of the continuum, is Lilith, who is partial to male flesh. It is Lilith, therefore, who embodies the possibility of liberation from Marian amorphousness. Lilith, murderess, murderess of males, and worst of all murderess of her own male issue (itself the supposed Freudian compensation for the lack of a penis which she apparently does not envy but does eat), is in effect the originator of two lines of descent: one male, finite and devoured; the other female, infinite and devouring. The infinite is associated with the many rather than with the single, is antithetical to the oneness of God, and carries menace as well as stigma (*Endres: 1993). As a punishment for this latter, irrepressible female line, Lilith is declared anathema: she is unwritten or proscribed from Scripture, erased and relegated to folklore.

In *Powers of Horror* (1982: 90–91) Kristeva offers a reading of the biblical preoccupation with the identification and exclusion of impurities. This preoccupation is rooted in a perception of the heterodox as an autonomous force threatening divine agency. The classification of heterodoxy as an abomination expresses the manner in which it departs from the Symbolic and thus prevents it from being actualized as demonic evil. Where such mechanisms fail, as is arguably the case in a story such as 'Natal na barca', and the

line separating Mary from Lilith dissolves, the maternal becomes demonic
and, by implication, annihilatory.

In the Bible, furthermore, the moment of criminal motherhood, whether
that of Lilith or Eve, is preceded by an equally dangerous desecration. In the
Garden of Eden the prohibition was applied to the fruit of two trees: that of
Knowledge and that of Life. When Adam and Eve partook of the fruit of the
Tree of Knowledge they were banished from Paradise lest they should proceed to eat of the fruit of the Tree of Life and become immortal, too. The
Judaeo-Christian God demarcates the boundaries between Himself (all-
knowing and immortal) and his creatures (ignorant and mortal). The pur-
loined knowledge enclosed in the apple represents the achievement by Eve of
a partial transgression which falls short of the theft of immortality. The fantasy of death-wielding powers, which is the power of immortality (and Lilith's
fantasy), has become a familiar trope for a series of women writers, and especially for Fagundes Telles.

The woman who wields death with impunity, in fiction as in life, usurps the
divine prerogative to do so and becomes, therefore, immortal. She is the recipient of male sacrifice and is herself god-like, albeit demonic rather than divine. In Fagundes Telles the mother does so, furthermore, by becoming the
mother/lover who biblically and traditionally appeared as the scapegoat for a
series of transgressions and divine reaffirmations and as such suffered death,
real or metaphorical. But in this writer's work the mother achieves the tri-
umph, also heretical, of immortality vis-à-vis male transience.

Thus monotheism is forced to surrender to Manichaeism, the profanity of
dual creation: God but also mother, Creator but also annihilator, not male
but female. The rise of the murderous mother mimics the rise of God the Father but, since the latter's permanence requires exclusivity, which is the rule of
the single Law, and since the simulacrum of motherly as opposed to Godly
creation introduces the heresy of the slightly different (the possibility of an alternative), the presence of the maternal renders itself heretical and jeopar-
dizes monotheistic paternity. When, in the works of Fagundes Telles,
monotheism gives way to Manichaean heresy, the prevailing demiurgic logic
suggests that the murder of sons and lovers becomes consecrated as sacrifice
to and within a new order. Kristeva argues that, biblically, abjection – the
mere exclusion of the other – gradually tempered and replaced the necessity
for blood sacrifice which disposed of that other in death. In the works of

Fagundes Telles, however, an economy of sacrifice is reinstated and the sacrificial lamb, newly identified as the male son, becomes not the reaffirmation of the single Law but the pretext for a new utterance with a heretical difference, the consequences of which may be apocalyptic for the established order.

In considering the phenomenon of women and, more specifically, mothers who kill, two things stand out. Firstly, there seems to be great difficulty in attempting to explain or even describe a woman who kills. Secondly, the impression persists that once a woman metamorphoses into a taker of life (and nothing short of metamorphosis seems to suffice as a half-way-house explanation for such an inexplicable act), no power can destroy her except her own or another woman's. Helen Birch (1993: 34 – 35) locates the killer woman at the heart of what she describes as a totemic storm between the forces of good and evil: she is an escapee from an overdetermined definition of acceptable femininity, polarized as its antithesis – the bad 'mother', the horrible dark face of femininity perverted from its natural course. There is no language for the murderous actions of such women (but not necessarily those of their male equivalents), particularly if the victims are children and, even more diabolically, their own children. In considering real-life female killers such as Myra Hindley and Rosemary West, the sheer horror of what confronts us usually entails, amid the avalanche of newspaper coverage, an even more profound explanatory silence. How could such a thing ever happen? How could a woman ever do it? The silence is possibly the consequence not of *not* knowing what to say but of *always* having known and of having wished not to: that the mother who gives life can also take it away; that the life force, the be-all of the infant, can also be its end-all; and that at the heart of the maternal there might lie violent dissolution.

If even the virginal Madonna can become a killer and, in 'Natal na barca', a speaking killer, a mother-turned-author on the theme of her infanticide, we have only the vocabulary of insanity, evil, and the lynch mob to respond to this phenomenon. But what that Nativity story, more explicitly than others, requires us to do is to ask ourselves whose son is killed, whose divine Child, whose offspring? When, in Fagundes Telles's stories, women turn themselves into the mothers of sons, and, less frequently, into the daughters of fathers, before they kill them (while still loving them), they go out of their way to commit the abominations of incest and the slaying of kin, both of which, according to both Greek and Judaeo-Christian ethics, have never gone unpunished, or almost never. In the case of this writer they remain unpunished, almost always.

Fagundes Telles's writing expresses the profane, the transgressive, the desecratory, and through her Lilith-like onslaughts upon the male she at once aborts, castrates, and kills, all actions which prematurely terminate life and pleasure. Abortion is the wrecking of the possibility of new life. Castration is the wrecking of the possibility of pleasure. Murder is the wrecking of the possibility of ongoing life or immortality. But they are all premature wreckages, untimely anticipations of the death which is, in every case, inherent in the moment when the mother, in giving life, gives finite life: life without the promise of perpetuity, eternity, or immortality. Life is poisoned, therefore: initiated by a birth quantitatively but not qualitatively different from its deformed avatars of abortion, castration, and murder, to which it is linked by the common denominator of ineluctable death. And, at the origin of this horrible truth, whether she be murderous or simply maternal, we find the mother: 'Mães há só uma'.

In his trips down psychic and mythical memory lane, Freud curiously omitted all mention of one destiny undoubtedly as striking as that of Oedipus, and certainly more disturbing. I refer to Euripides's Medea: witch, sorceress, demon-woman, and, finally, childkiller and slayer of her own kin. Having destroyed her children in order to wreak revenge upon their father, and in particular upon his line, Medea exits with impunity to go and live in peace in, of all places, Athens, the seat of masculinely conceived Justice. Aristotle admired Euripides as the most tragic of the Greek poets because he was purveyor of the unhappiest endings (Aristotle 1965: 48–49). He was certainly the most controversial, and he was reviled by contemporaries such as Aristophanes (1993) or dismissed by them. Euripides portrays that most unsympathetic of roles, the unspeakably bad mother, sympathetically and, by denying his audience the catharsis of retribution, allows the effects of disruption to endure.

The woman who kills children, let alone her own (who are, for Freud and within the parameters of Greek Antiquity, her lovers), unsettles the boundary of what is knowable about femininity as the 'guarantor of idealism, nurturance (sic), and nature', and invites instead a glimpse into its abysmal antithesis (Birch 1993: 53). Ultimately, what is unhinged in the process is knowledge, the knowledge that was thought to be available and which, since Eve desecrated the Tree, has always been the real target of onslaught. Over-whelmingly, throughout Fagundes Telles's fiction, the limits of female gnosis encompass not the consciousness of the mortality of self and other, but the more portentous knowledge of how to kill with impunity. Fagundes Telles in-augurates a permanent suspension of the Law-of-the-Father and enacts repli-cas of a variety of erstwhile sacred rituals with a small heretical difference: boastful confession without contrition, triumphalist evil rather than repenting sin, 'the joy of ... dissipation set into signs' (Kristeva 1982: 131), the path that stays 'within horror but at a very slight distance – an infinitesimal and tremen-dous one ... writing as sublimation' (144). It is writing as indefinite catharsis (208), or, to put it differently, as an act of aesthetic *coitus interruptus*, which as everyone knows dislocates a number of orthodoxies: fertilizing, reproductive, proprietorial, pleasurable, and other.

If, as Edward Said maintains, inherent in the concept of writing is the con-cept of authoritative fathering, Fagundes Telles, writing as a woman in Brazil (whose problematic birth has its origin in the rapacious expansionism of at least one and probably several European mothers – androgynous 'pátrias' or 'mátrias'), appears as the mother, not the 'authoring' father, of terrifying texts which disclose a dual impetus towards enlightenment and indictment.[3] En-lightenment, commensurate with the consciousness of death, is the final en-counter which has been longed for and, semiotically and symbolically, for-gone. Indictment is resident in the insistence and lament that, for the mo-ment, at the heart of a female voice, of this female voice, there lies the imper-ative and the limitation of being compelled to peer into the vacuum of the soul and from it to extract the only available measure of lyricism: evil recol-lected in tranquillity.

MARIA MANUEL LISBOA

St John's College, Cambridge

---

3.   For a discussion of this, see Gilbert & Gubar (1984: 3–4).

BIBLIOGRAPHY

Apuleius (1988). *Metamorfosis o El asno de oro*, tr. Diego López de Cortegana (1513? 1525?), ed. Carlos García Gual (Madrid: Alianza).

Arenal, Electa & Stacey Schlau (1989a). *Untold Sisters: Hispanic Nuns in their Own Works*, tr. Amanda Powell (Albuquerque: University of New Mexico Press).

Arenal, Electa & Stacey Schlau (1989b). ' "Leyendo yo y escribiendo ella": The Convent as Intellectual Community', *Journal of Hispanic Philology* 13: 214–29.

Aristophanes (1993). *Frogs*, ed. Kenneth James Dover (Oxford: Clarendon Press).

Aristotle (1965). *Classical Literary Criticism: Aristotle On the Art of Poetry, Horace On the Art of Poetry, Longinus On the Sublime*, ed. & tr. T. S. Dorsch (Harmondsworth: Penguin), 29–75.

Atencia, María Victoria (1990). *La señal: Poesía 1969–1989*, ed. Rafael León (Malaga: Ayuntamiento de Málaga).

Augustine, St (1995). *De doctrina christiana*, ed. R. P. H. Green, Oxford Early Christian Texts (Oxford: Clarendon Press).

Ayala-Dip, J. Ernesto (1994). Review of Cristina Fernández Cubas, *Con Ágatha en Estambul*, *El País* (21 May): 10.

Bachelard, Gaston (1943). *L'Air et les songes: Essai sur l'imagination du mouvement* (Paris: José Corti; repr. 1970).

Bachelard, Gaston (1971). *La Poétique de la rêverie*, Bibliothèque de philosophie contemporaine: Logique et philosophie des sciences (Paris: Presses Universitaires de France; first edn 1960).

Barbero, Teresa (1967). *El último verano en el espejo*, Colección Áncora y delfín 301 (Barcelona: Destino).

Barthes, Roland (1977a). 'The Death of the Author', in Heath (1977: 142–48). First publ. as 'La mort de l'auteur', *Montéia* 5 (1968).

Barthes, Roland (1977b). 'From Work to Text', in Heath (1977: 155–64); also in Harari (1980: 73–81). First publ. as 'De l'oeuvre au texte', *Revue d'esthétique* 3 (1971).

Bataille, Georges (1985). 'Emily Brontë', in his *Literature and Evil*, tr. Alastair Hamilton (London & New York: Marion Boyars), 13–31, First British edn, Signature Series (London: Calder & Boyars, 1973). First publ. as *Le littérature et le mal: Emily Bronte, Baudelaire, Michelet, Blake, Sade, Proust, Kafka, Genet* (Paris: Gallimard, 1957).

Baudrillard, Jean (1988). 'Simulacra and Simulations', tr. Paul Foss, Paul Patton, & Philip Beitchman, in *Jean Baudrillard: Selected Writings*, ed. Mark Poster (Cambridge: Polity Press & Oxford: Blackwell), 166–84.

Baudrillard, Jean (1993). 'Whatever Happened to Evil?', in *The Transparency of Evil: Essays on Extreme Phenomena*, tr. James Benedict (London & New York: Verso), 81–88. First publ. as *La Transparence du mal: Essai sur les phénomènes extrêmes*, L'Espace critique (Paris: Éditions Galilée, 1990).

Beauvoir, Simone de (1964). *The Second Sex*, tr. Howard Madison Parshley (New York: Knopf). First British edn London: Jonathan Cape, 1953.

Bellver, Catherine G. (1982). 'Two New Women Writers from Spain', *Letras femeninas*, 8/ii: 3–7.

Bellver, Catherine G. (1991). Review of Cristina Fernández Cubas, *El ángulo del horror*, *Letras peninsulares*, 4: 371–73.

Bellver, Catherine G. (1992). '*El año de Gracia* and the Displacement of the Word', *Studies in Twentieth-Century Literature* 16: 221–32.

Bettelheim, Bruno (1985). *The Uses of Enchantment: The Meaning and Importance of Fairy-Tales* (New York: Knopf; first edn 1976). First British edn. London: Thames & Hudson, 1976.

Birch, Helen (ed.) (1993). *Moving Targets: Women, Murder, and Representation* (London: Virago).

Botana, Alicia V. (1994). Review of Cristina Fernández Cubas, *Con Ágatha en Estambul*, *El Mundo* (11 June), unpaginated.

Bretz, Mary Lee (1988). 'Cristina Fernández Cubas and the Recuperation of the Semiotic in *Los altillos de Brumal*', *Anales de la literatura española contemporánea* 13: 177–88.

Brivic, Sheldon R. (1991). *The Veil of Signs: Joyce, Lacan, and Perception*, Illini Books (Urbana IL: University of Illinois Press).

Brown, Joan Lipman & Crista Johnson (1995). 'The Contemporary Hispanic Novel: Is There a Canon?', *Hispania* 78: 252–61.

Brown, Joan Lipman (1991). 'Women Writers of Spain: An Historical Perspective', in *Women Writers of Contemporary Spain: Exiles in the Homeland*, ed. Joan Lipman Brown (London & Toronto: Delaware University Press & Associated University Presses), 13–25.

Bynum, Caroline Walker (1982). *Jesus as Mother: Studies in the Spirituality of the High Middle Ages* (Berkeley CA, Los Angeles, & London: University of California Press).

Bynum, Caroline Walker (1987). *Holy Feast and Holy Fast: The Religious Significance of Food to Medieval Women*, The New Historicism: Studies in Cultural Poetics (Berkeley CA, Los Angeles, & London: University of California Press).

Cano, Melchor (1871). 'Censura del Catecismo de B. Carranza (1563)', in Fermín Agosto Caballero, *Conquenses ilustres*, 4 vols (Madrid: Oficina Tipográfica del Hospicio, 1868–75), II: *Vida del illustríssimo Sr D. Melchor Cano*.

Cervantes Saavedra, Miguel de (1969). *Los trabajos de Persiles y Sigismunda* (1617), ed. Juan Bautista Avalle-Arce, Clásicos Castalia 12 (Madrid: Castalia; repr. 1978, etc.).

Céspedes y Meneses, Gonzalo de (1975). *Varia fortuna del soldado Píndaro* (1626), ed. Arsenio Pacheco, 2 vols, Clásicos castellanos 202–03 (Madrid: Espasa-Calpe).

Charnon-Deutsch, Lou (1991). 'The Sexual Economy in the Narrative of María de Zayas', *Letras femeninas* 17: 15–28.

Chodorow, Nancy (1979). *The Reproduction of Mothering: Psychoanalysis and the Sociology of Gender* (Berkeley CA, Los Angeles, & London: University of California Press).

Ciplijauskaité, Biruté (1993). 'Memoria, historia, *yo*: Variaciones femeninas/masculinas', *La Torre* 7: 339–54.

Cixous, Hélène (1972). *The Exile of James Joyce*, tr. Sally A. J. Purcell (New York: David Lewis). First publ. as *Exil de James Joyce, ou l'art du remplacement*, Publications de la Faculté des Lettres et Sciences Humaines de Paris–Sorbonne: Série Recherches 46 (Paris: B. Grasset, 1968).

Cixous, Hélène & Catherine Clément (1994). 'Sorties: Out and Out: Attacks/Ways Out/Forays', in *The Newly Born Woman: Hélène Cixous et Catherine Clément*, ed. Sandra Mortola Gilbert, tr. Betsy Wing (London: I. B. Tauris), 61–132; second edn, Theory and History of Literature 24 (Manchester: Manchester University Press, 1986). First publ. in French in 1975.

Cixous, Hélène (1981). 'Castration or Decapitation' ed. & tr. Annette Kuhn, *Signs* 2/i: 41–55.

Cixous, Hélène (1992). 'Writing and the Law: Blanchot, Joyce, Kafka, and Lispector', in her *Readings: The Poetics of Blanchot, Joyce, Kafka, Kleist, Lispector, and Tsvetayeva*, ed. & tr. Verena Andermatt Conley (New York & London: Harvester Wheatsheaf), 1–27.

Cook, Albert Spaulding (1993). *Canons and Wisdoms* (Philadelphia PA: University of Pennsylvania Press).

Costa, Luis (1991). 'Women in Franco's Spain', in *The Sea of Becoming: Approaches to the Fiction of Esther Tusquets*, ed. Mary Seale Vasquez (Westport CT: Greenwood Press), 10–28.

Deyermond, Alan (1976–77). '"El convento de dolençias": The Works of Teresa de Cartagena', *Journal of Hispanic Philology* 1: 19–29.

Deyermond, Alan (1983). 'Spain's First Women Writers', in *Women in Hispanic Literature: Icons and Fallen Idols*, ed. Beth Kurti Miller (Berkeley CA: University of California Press), 27–52.

Díaz, Janet Winecoff (1971). 'The Trilogy, *Los mercaderes* (The Merchants)', in her *Ana María Matute*, Twayne's World Authors Series 152 (New York: Twayne Publishers), 130–43.

Dinnerstein, Dorothy (1987). *The Rocking of the Cradle, and the Ruling of the World* (London: The Women's Press). First publ. as *The Mermaid and the Minotaur: The Rocking of the Cradle, and the Ruling of the World* (New York: Harper & Row, 1976).

Dowling, Colette (1981). *The Cinderella Complex: Women's Hidden Fear of Independence* (New York: Summit Books; repr. London: Michael Joseph, 1982).

Eliade, Mircea (1958). *Birth and Rebirth*, tr. Willard Ropes Trask (London: Harper & Brohers). Repr. as *Symbols of Initiation: The Mysteries of Birth and Rebirth*, Harper Torch Books TB 12364 (New York: Harper & Row, 1965).

Ellis, Deborah Sue (1981). 'The Image of the Home in Early English and Spanish Literature' (unpubl. diss., University of California at Berkeley).

Endres, Frank Carl (1993). *The Mystery of Numbers*, tr. & rev. Annemarie Schimmel (New York & Oxford: Oxford University Press). First publ. as *Das Mysterium der Zahl*.

Erasmus, Desiderius (1910). *Ciceronianus* (1528), ed. & tr. Izora Scott in *Controversies over the Imitation of Cicero as a Model for Style and Some Phases of their Influence on the Schools of the Renaissance*, Columbia Teachers College Contributions to Education 35 (New York: Teachers College, Columbia University; repr. Davis CA: Hermagoras Press, 1961).

Fernández Cubas, Cristina (1980). *Mi hermana Elba*, Cuadernos ínfimos 92 (Barcelona: Tusquets).

Fernández Cubas, Cristina (1983). *Los altillos de Brumal*, Cuadernos ínfimos 112 (Barcelona: Tusquets).

Fernández Cubas, Cristina (1985). *El año de Gracia*, Colección Andanzas 20 (Barcelona: Tusquets).

Fernández Cubas, Cristina (1990). *El ángulo del horror*, Fabula 54 (Barcelona: Tusquets).

Fernández Cubas, Cristina (1994). *Con Ágatha en Estambul*, Colección Andanzas 213 (Barcelona: Tusquets).

Fetterley, Judith, 1978. *The Resisting Reader: A Feminist Approach to American Fiction* (Bloomington IN: Indiana University Press; repr. 1981).

Fitz, Earl E. (1985). *Clarice Lispector*, Twayne's World Authors Series 755 (Boston: Twayne Publishers).

Flandrin, Jean-Louis (1979). *Families in Former Times: Kinship, Household, and Sexuality*, tr. Richard Southern (Cambridge, etc.: Cambridge University Press).

Fleenor, Juliann E. (ed.) (1983). *The Female Gothic* (Montreal & London: Eden Press).

Foa, Sandra M. (1978). 'María de Zayas: Visión conflictiva y renuncia del mundo', *Cuadernos Hispanoamericanos* 111/cccxxxi: 128–35.

Foster, David William (1966). '*Nada* de Carmen Laforet: Ejemplo de neo-romance en la novela contemporánea', in *Novelistas españoles de postguerra*, ed. Rodolfo Cardona, El escritor y la crítica–Persiles 96 (Madrid: Taurus, 1976), 89–104. First publ. *Revista Hispánica Moderna* 32 (1966): 43–55.

Foucault, Michel (1980). 'What Is an Author?', in Harari (1980: 141–60).

Franz, Marie-Luise von (1970). *An Introduction to the Interpretation of Fairy-Tales*, Seminar Series 1 (Dallas TX: Spring Publications; repr. 1987). Based on lectures given in 1963 at the C.G. Jung Institute, Zürich.

Freud, Sigmund (1961a). 'Some Psychical Consequences of the Anatomical Distinction Between the Sexes' (1925), in *The Standard Edition of the Complete Psychological Works*, ed. & tr. James Strachey, Anna Freud, & Carrie Lee Rothgels, 24 vols (London: Hogarth Press & The Institute of Psycho-Analysis), XIX: 241–60.

Freud, Sigmund (1961b). 'Female Sexuality' (1931), in *The Standard Edition*, XXI: 221–46.

Freud, Sigmund (1964). 'Masculinity and Femininity', in *The Standard Edition*, XXII: 113–17.

Freud, Sigmund (1983). *The Interpretation of Dreams*, ed. & tr. James Strachey, The Pelican Freud Library 4 (Harmondsworth: Penguin; first edn 1976).

Furman, Nelly (1985). 'The Politics of Language: Beyond the Gender Principle?', in Greene & Kahn (1985: 58–79).

Gilbert, Sandra Mortola & Susan Gubar (1979). *The Madwoman in the Attic: The Woman Writer and the Nineteenth-Century Literary Imagination* (New Haven CT: Yale University Press; repr. 1989 etc.; second edn 1984).

Glenn, Kathleen M. (1992). 'Gothic indecipherability and Doubling in the Fiction of Cristina Fernández Cubas', *Monographic Review/Revista monográfica* 8: 125–41.

Glenn, Kathleen M. (1993). 'Conversación con Cristina Fernández Cubas', *Anales de la literatura española contemporánea* 18: 355–63.

Gleue, Julie (1992). 'The Epistemological and Ontological Implications in Cristina Fernández Cubas's *El año de Gracia'*, *Monographic Review/Revista monográfica* 8: 142–56.

Gourman, Jack (1989). *The Gourman Report: A Rating of Graduate and Professional Programmes in American and International Universities*, 5th edn (Los Angeles CA: National Education Standards).

Goytisolo, Juan (1977). 'El mundo erótico de María de Zayas', in his *Disidencias*, Biblioteca breve 426 (Barcelona: Seix Barral), 63–115. First publ. *Cuadernos de Ruedo Ibérico* 39/40 (1972).

Greene, Gayle & Coppélia Kahn (eds) (1985). *Making a Difference: Feminist Literary Criticism* (New York & London: Methuen).

Guillén, Claudio (1957). 'Estilística del silencio (en torno a un poema de Antonio Machado)', *Revista hispánica moderna* 23: 260–91.

Guillory, John (1993). *Cultural Capital: The Problem of Literary Canon Formation* (Chicago IL & London: University of Chicago Press).

Haggerty, George E. (1989). *Gothic Fiction/Gothic Form* (University Park PA & London: Pennsylvania State University Press).

Hahner, June Edith (1990). *Emancipating the Female Sex: The Struggle for Women's Rights in Brazil, 1850–1940* (Durham NC & London: Duke University Press).

Harari, Josué V. (ed.) (1980). *Textual Strategies: Perspectives in Post-Structuralist Criticism* (London: Methuen & Co. Ltd; first edn, New York: Cornell University Press, 1979).

Harris, Wendell V. (1991). 'Canonicity', *Publications of the Modern Language Association of America* 106: 110–21.

Heath, Stephen (ed. & tr.) (1977). *Roland Barthes: Image, Music, Text*, Fontana Communications (London: Fontana; repr. 1982, etc.).

Hart, Stephen M. (1993). *White Ink: Essays on Twentieth-Century Feminine Fiction in Spain and Latin America*, Colección Tamesis A 156 (London: Tamesis Books).

Henke, Suzette A. (1990). *James Joyce and the Politics of Desire* (New York & London: Routledge).

Hevia, Francisco de (1981). *Itinerario de la oración* (1553), ed. Manuel de Castro, Espirituales españoles A 29 (Madrid: Universidad Pontificia de Salamanca & Fundación Universitaria Española).

Holt, Marion P. (1992). 'Twentieth-Century Spanish Theatre and the Canon(s)', *Anales de la literatura española contemporánea* 17: 47–54.

Huélamo San José, Ana María (1992). 'El devocionario de la domínica Sor Constanza', *Boletín de la Asociación Española de Archiveros, Bibliotecarios, Museólogos y Documentalistas* 42: 133–47.

Ichiishi, Barbara Franklin (1994). *The Apple of Earthly Love: Female Development in Esther Tusquets's Fiction*, Nuestra voz 1 (New York: Peter Lang).

Jackson, Rosemary (1981). *Fantasy: The Literature of Subversion*, New Accents (London & New York: Methuen & Co.; repr. London: Routledge, 1988 etc.).

James, Sibyl (1983). 'Gothic Transformations: Isak Dinesen and the Gothic', in Fleenor (1983: 138–52).

Jones, Ann, Rosalind (1985). 'Inscribing Femininity: French Theories of the Feminine', in
    Greene & Kahn (1985: 80 – 112).
Jones, Margaret W. (1968). 'Religious Motifs and Biblical Allusions in the Works of Ana
    María Matute', *Hispania* 51: 416 – 23.
Joyce, James (1993). 'The Dead', in *A James Joyce Reader*, ed. Harry Levin, Penguin 20th-
    Century Classics (Harmondsworth: Penguin).

Kearney, Richard (1988). *The Wake of Imagination: Ideas of Creativity in Western Culture*,
    Problems of Modern European Thought (London: Hutchinson).
Kearney, Richard (1991). *Poetics of Imagining: From Husserl to Lyotard*, Problems of Modern
    European Thought (London: Harper Collins Academic; repr. London: Routledge, 1993).
Klobucka, Anna (1994). 'Hélène Cixous and the Hour of Clarice Lispector', *Substance* 73:
    41 – 62.
Kolbenschlag, Madonna (1979). *Kiss Sleeping Beauty Goodbye: Breaking the Spell of Feminine
    Myths and Models* (Garden City, New York: Doubleday; repr. Dublin: Arlen House,
    1983; second edn San Francisco CA: Harper Row, 1988).
Kristeva, Julia (1981). 'Word, Dialogue, and Novel', in *Desire in Language: A Semiotic Ap-
    proach to Literature and Art*, ed. Leon S. Roudiez, tr. Thomas Gora, Alice Jardine, & Leon
    S. Roudiez (Oxford: Blackwell), 64 – 91. First edn New York: Columbia University Press,
    1980.
Kristeva, Julia (1982). *Powers of Horror: An Essay on Abjection*, tr. Léon S. Roudiez,
    European Perspectives (New York & Oxford: Columbia University Press). First publ. as
    Pouvoirs de l'horreur: Essai sur l'abjection, Tel Quel (Paris: Éditions du Seuil, 1980).
Kristeva, Julia (1993). 'About Chinese Women', in *The Kristeva Reader*, ed. Toril Moi (Oxford:
    Basil Blackwell). Essay first publ. 1986.

Laforet, Carmen (1944). *Nada*, Colección Áncora y delfín 27 (Barcelona: Destino; repr. 1947
    etc.).
Laplanche, Jean & Jean-Bertrand Pontalis (1986). 'Fantasy and the Origins of Sexuality', in
    Formations of Fantasy, ed. Victor Burgin, James Donald, & Cora Kaplan (London & New
    York: Methuen; repr. 1989 etc.), 5 – 34.
Laurent, Marie-Hyacinthe (ed.) (1936). *Documenti*, Fontes Vitae S. Catharinae Senensis His-
    torici 1 (Siena: Reale Università di Siena, Cattedra Cateriniana).
Lauter, Paul (1991). *Canons and Contexts* (New York & Oxford: Oxford University Press).
Leonard, Garry (1991). 'Joyce and Lacan: "The Woman" as Symptom of "Masculinity" in
    "The Dead" ', *James Joyce Quarterly* 28: 451 – 72.
Levine, Linda Gould (1983). 'Carmen Martín Gaite's *El cuarto de atrás*: A Portrait of the
    Artist as Woman', in Servodidio & Welles (1983: 162 – 72).
Lispector, Clarice. (1980). 'A Partida do Trem' in her *Onde Estivestes de Noite* (Rio de
    Janeiro: Nova Fronteira; first edn Rio de Janeiro: Artenova, 1974).
López Estrada, Francisco (1986). 'Las mujeres escritoras en la Edad Media castellana', in *La
    condición de la mujer en la Edad Media: Actas del Coloquio celebrado en la Casa de
    Velázquez del 5 al 7 de noviembre de 1984*, ed. Yves-Ren Fonquerne & Alfonso Esteban,
    Coloquio hispano-francés 3 (Madrid: Casa de Velázquez & Universidad Complutense),
    9 – 38.

Luis, de Granada (1855). *Libro de la oración y consideración*, in *Obras completas*, ed. José Joaquín de Mora, 3rd edn, 3 vols, Biblioteca de Autores Españoles 6 8 11 (Madrid: Rivadeneyra), II: 1–202.

Luis, de Granada (1908). *Obras de fray Luis de Granada*, ed. Justo Cuervo, 14 vols (Madrid: Imprenta de la Viuda e Hija de Gómez Fuentenebro), XIV: *Doctrina espiritual*.

Luna, Pedro de (1884). *Libro de las consolaciones de la vida humana*, ed. Pascual de Gayangos, Biblioteca de Autores Españoles 51 (= *Escritores en prosa anteriores al siglo XV*) (Madrid: Sucesores de Hernando), 561–602. First publ. Madrid: M. Rivadeneyra, 1860.

Machado, Antonio (1952). *Poesías completas*, Colección Austral 149, 6th edn (Buenos Aires: Espasa-Calpe).

McLaughlin, Eleanor Commo (1974). 'Equality of Souls, Inequality of Sexes: Women in Medieval Theology', in *Religion and Sexism: Images of Woman in the Jewish and Christian Traditions*, ed. Rosemary Ruether (New York: Simon & Schuster), 213–66.

Margenot, John B. III (1993). 'Parody and Self-Consciousness in Cristina Fernández Cubas's *El año de Gracia*', *Siglo XX/20th Century* 11: 71–87.

Marimón Llorca, Carmen (1990). 'Teresa de Cartagena', in his *Prosistas castellanas medievales*, Publicaciones de la Caja de Ahorros de la Excma Diputación de Alicante 153 (Alicante: Caja de Ahorros Provincial), 102–34.

Maroto Camino, Mercedes (1994). '*Spindles for Swords*: The Re-Discovery of María de Zayas's Presence', *Hispanic Review* 62: 519–36.

Martín Gaite, Carmen (1958). *Entre visillos*, Colección Áncora y delfín 147 (Barcelona: Destino).

Martín Gaite, Carmen (1978). *El cuarto de atrás*, Colección Áncora y delfín 530 (Barcelona: Ediciones Destino).

Martín Gaite, Carmen (1986). *Dos relatos fantásticos*, Palabra en el tiempo 170 (Barcelona: Lumen).

Martín Gaite, Carmen (1994). *La reina de las nieves*, Narrativas hispánicas 163 (Barcelona: Editorial Anagrama).

Martin, Stephen-Paul (1988). *Open Form and the Feminine Imagination: The Politics of Reading in Twentieth-Century Innovative Writing*, Postmodern Positions 2 (Washington DC: Maisonneuve Press).

Masoliver Ródenas, Juan Antonio (1994). Review of Cristina Fernández Cubas, *Con Ágatha en Estambul*, *La Vanguardia* (3 June).

Matute, Ana María (1960). *Primera memoria*, Coleccion Destinolibro 7 (Barcelona: Destino); repr., Colección Áncora y delfín 179 (Barcelona: Destino, 1961).

Matute, Ana María (1961). *Tres y un sueño* (Barcelona: Destino).

Merleau-Ponty, Maurice (1945). *Phénoménologie de la perception*, 8th edn, Bibliothèque des idées (Paris: Gallimard).

Miles, Rosalind (1989). *The Women's History of the World* (London: Paladin; first edn London: Michael Joseph, 1988).

Mirrer, Louise (1989). 'Feminist Approaches to Medieval Spanish History and Literature', *Medieval Feminist Newsletter* 7: 2–7.

Mitchell, Juliet & Jacqueline Rose (eds) (1982). *Feminine Sexuality: Jacques Lacan and the École freudienne*, tr. Jacqueline Rose (Basingstoke: Macmillan).

Moi, Toril (1985). *Sexual/Textual Politics: Feminist Literary Theory*, New Accents (London & New York: Methuen).

Molina, Irene Alejandra (1990). 'La *Arboleda de los enfermos* de Teresa de Cartagena: Un sermón consolatorio olvidado' (unpubl. MA dissertation, University of Texas at Austin).

Muecke, Douglas Colin (1982). *Irony and the Ironic*, second edn., rev., The Critical Idiom 13 (London & New York: Methuen & Co Ltd; first edn 1970, etc.).

Norris, Margot. (1994). 'Not the Girl She Was at All: Women in "The Dead" ', in Schwarz (1994: 190–205).

Ortega, José (1992). 'La dimensión fantástica en los cuentos de Fernández Cubas', *Monographic Review/Revista monográfica* 8: 157–63.

Ortega y Gasset, José (1912). 'Antonio Machado: "Campos de Castilla" ', in *Ensayos sobre la generación del '98 y otros escritores españoles contemporáneos*, ed. Paulino Garagorri, Obras de José Ortega y Gasset (Madrid: Revista del Occidente en Alianza, 1981), 275–80.

Ortega y Gasset, José (1924). 'Vitalidad, alma, espíritu', in *El espectador* (Madrid: Biblioteca Nueva, 1950), 611–55.

Ostriker, Alicia (1986). 'The Thieves of Language: Women Poets and Revisionist Mythmaking', in *The New Feminist Criticism: Essays on Women, Literature, and Theory*, ed. Elaine Showalter (London: Virago), 314–38. First publ. *Signs* 8 (1981).

Pérez Firmat, Gustavo (1991). 'Carmen Laforet: The Dilemma of Artistic Vocation', in Brown (1991: 26–41).

Pérez, Janet (1995). 'Structural, Thematic and Symbolic Mirrors in *El cuarto de atrás* and *Nubosidad variable* of Martín Gaite', *South Central Review*, 12/i: 47–63.

Peterson's Guide to Graduate Programes in the Humanities and Social Sciences, 1991 (1990), 25th edn (Princeton NJ: Peterson's Guides), 589–620.

Petrarch (1966). *Letters*, tr. Morris Bishop (Bloomington IN: Indiana University Press).

Pigman, G. W. III (1980). 'Versions of Imitation in the Renaissance', *Renaissance Quarterly* 33: 1–32.

Place, Edwin B. (1923). *María de Zayas: An Outstanding Woman Short-Story Writer of Seventeenth-Century Spain*, University of Colorado Studies 13 (Boulder CO: University of Colorado Press).

Rich, Adrienne Cecile (1992). *Of Woman Born: Motherhood as Experience and Institution* (London: Virago; first edn 1977). First publ. New York: W. W. Norton, 1976.

Riera, Carme & Luisa Cotoner (1987). 'Los personajes femeninos de doña María de Zayas: Una aproximación', in *Literatura y vida cotidiana: Actas de las cuartas jornadas de investigación interdisciplinar organizadas por el Seminario de estudios de la mujer de la Universidad Autónoma de Madrid*, ed. José Antonio Rey del Corral, Colección del Seminario de estudios de la mujer 11 (Zaragoza: Universidad de Zaragoza), 149–59.

Riquelme, John Paul (1994). 'For Whom the Snow Taps: Style and Repetition in "The Dead" ', in Schwarz (1994: 219–233).

Rodríguez Rivas, Gregorio (1992). 'La *Arboleda de los enfermos* de Teresa de Cartagena: Literatura ascética en el siglo XV', *Entemu* 3: 117–30.

Salinas, Pedro (1971). *Poesías completas*, ed. Soledad Salinas de Marichal, prol. Jorge Guillén, Biblioteca crítica (Barcelona: Barral).

Sanz, María (1986). 'Poemas', in *Litoral femenino: Literatura escrita por mujeres en la España contemporánea*, ed. Lorenzo Saval & Jesús García Gallego (Madrid: Revista Litoral), 223–24.

Sanz, María (1988). *Contemplaciones*, Taifa poesía 18 (Barcelona: Taifa).

Sanz, María (1991a). *Los aparecidos*, Poesía 8 (Guadalajara: Excma Diputación Provincial).

Sanz, María (1991b). *Pétalo impar (Antología 1981–1991)*, Adonais 486 (Madrid: Rialp).

Scheler, Max (1957). 'Ordo amoris', in his *Schriften aus dem Nachlass*, ed. Maria Scheler, 3 vols, Gesammelte Werke 10–13 (Bern: Francke), I: 347–76.

Schwarz, Daniel R. (ed.) (1994). *James Joyce: 'The Dead': Complete, Authoritative Text with Biographical and Historical Contexts, Critical History, and Essays from Five Contemporary Cultural Perspectives*, Case Studies in Contemporary Criticism (Boston MA & New York: Bedford Books of St Martin's Press).

Seidenspinner-Núñez, Dayle (1994). ' "Él sólo me leyó": Gendered Hermeneutics and Subversive Poetics in the *Admiraçión operum Dey* of Teresa de Cartagena', *Medievalia* 15: 14-23.

Servodidio, Mirella d'Ambrosio (1983). 'Oneiric Intertextualities', in Servodidio & Welles (1983: 117–27).

Servodidio, Mirella d'Ambrosio & Marcia L. Welles (eds) (1983). *From Fiction to Metafiction: Essays in Honor of Carmen Martín Gaite* (Lincoln NA: Society of Spanish and Spanish-American Studies).

Santa Teresa, Silverio de OCD (ed.) (1935). *Procesos de beatificación y canonización de Santa Teresa de Jesús*, 3 vols, Obras de Santa Teresa 1–3: Biblioteca mística carmelitana 18–20 (Burgos: Monte Carmelo).

Smith, Paul Julian (1989). *The Body Hispanic: Gender and Sexuality in Spanish and Spanish-American Narrative* (Oxford: Clarendon Press).

Stallybrass, Peter (1986). 'Patriarchal Territories: The Body Enclosed', in *Rewriting the Renaissance: The Discourses of Sexual Difference in Early Modern Europe*, ed. Margaret W. Ferguson, Maureen Quilligan, & Nancy J. Vickers, Women in Culture and Society (Chicago IL: University of Chicago Press; repr. 1987), 123–42.

Surtz, Ronald E. (1987). 'Image Patterns in Teresa de Cartagena's *Arboleda de los enfermos*', in *LA CHISPA '87: Selected Proceedings, The Eighth Louisiana Conference on Hispanic Languages and Literatures, Tulane University, New Orleans, 1981*, ed. Gilbert Paolini (New Orleans LA: Tulane University), 297–304.

Surtz, Ronald E. (1995). *Writing Women in Late Medieval and Early-Modern Spain: The Mothers of Saint Teresa of Avila*, Middle Ages Series (Philadelphia PA: University of Pennsylvania Press).

Talbot, Lynn K. (1989). 'Journey into the Fantastic: Cristina Fernández Cubas's *"Los altillos de Brumal"*', *Letras femeninas* 15: 37–47.

Telles, Lygia Fagundes (1984b). *Seminário dos ratos* (Rio de Janeiro: Nova Fronteira).

Telles, Lygia Fagundes (1981). *Mistérios: Ficções* (Rio de Janeiro: Editora Nova Fronteira).

Telles, Lygia Fagundes (1984a). *Os melhores contos de Lygia Fagundes Telles* (São Paulo: Global).

Telles, Lygia Fagundes (1986). *Antes do baile verde: Contos* (Rio de Janeiro: Nova Fronteira).

Teresa de Cartagena (1967). *Arboleda de los enfermos y Admiraçión operum Dey*, ed. Lewis Joseph Hutton, Anejos del Boletín de la Real Academia Española 16 (Madrid: Real Academia Española).

Teresa de Jesús, St (1965). *Camino de perfección*, facsimile edn, ed. Tomás Álvarez, 2 vols (Rome: Teresianum).

Teresa de Jesús, St (1978). *Constituciones*, facsimile edn, ed. Tomás Álvarez (Burgos: Monte Carmelo).

Teresa de Jesús, St (1986). *Camino de perfección*, first version (Escorial Codex = CE) and second version (Valladolid Codex = CV), in *Obras completas de Santa Teresa*, ed. Efrén de la Madre de Dios OCD & Otger Steggink (Madrid: BAC), 233–419.

Todorov, Tzvetan (1970). *Introduction à la littérature fantastique*, Politique (Paris: Éditions du Seuil); repr., Collection Points 73 (Paris: Éditions du Seuil, 1976).

Tusquets, Esther (1978). *El mismo mar de todos los veranos*, Palabra 50 (Barcelona: Lumen; repr. 1983).

Ugalde, Sharon Keefe (1991). *Conversaciones y poemas: La nueva poesía femenina española en castellano*, Lingüística y teoría literaria (Madrid: Siglo XXI de España).

Vicente García, Luis Miguel (1989). 'La defensa de la mujer como intelectual en Teresa de Cartagena y Sor Juana Inés de la Cruz', *Mester* 18: 95–103.

Vincent, Sybil Korff (1983). 'The Mirror and the Cameo: Margaret Atwood's Comic/Gothic Novel *Lady Oracle*', in Fleenor (1983: 153–63).

Waelti-Walters, Jennifer R. (1982). *Fairy-Tales and the Female Imagination* (Montreal: Eden Press).

Warner, Marina (1976). *Alone of All Her Sex: The Myth and Cult of the Virgin Mary* (London: Weidenfeld & Nicolson; repr. London: Picador, 1985).

Waugh, Patricia (1984). *Metafiction: The Theory and Practice of Self-Conscious Fiction* (London & New York: Methuen).

Waugh, Patricia (1989). *Feminine Fictions: Revisiting the Postmodern* (London: Routledge).

Welles, Marcia L. (1978). 'María de Zayas y Sotomayor and her *Novela Cortesana*: A Re-Evaluation', *Bulletin of Hispanic Studies* 55: 301–10.

Williamsen, Amy (1991). 'Engendering Interpretation: Irony as Comic Challenge in María de Zayas', *Romance Languages Annual* 3: 642–48.

Wilson, Diana de Armas (1994). 'Homage to Apuleius: Cervantes' Avenging Psyche', in *The Search for the Ancient Novel*, ed. James Tatum (Baltimore & London: The Johns Hopkins University Press), 88–100. A selection of papers read at the 1989 Durham–NEH International Conference 'The Ancient Novel: Classical Paradigms and Modern Perspectives'.

Zambrano, María (1950a). 'Apuntes sobre el tiempo y la poesía', in Zambrano (1950d: 32–35).

Zambrano, María (1950b). 'Hacia un saber sobre el alma', in Zambrano (1950d: 13–23).

Zambrano, María (1950c). 'La metáfora del corazón', in *Hacia un saber sobre el alma*, in Zambrano (1950d: 41–49).

Zambrano, María (1950d). *Hacia un saber sobre el alma*, Biblioteca filosófica (Buenos Aires: Losada).

Zambrano, María (1971). 'El sueño creador', in her *Obras reunidas* (Madrid: Aguilar), 15–112.

Zatlin, Phyllis (1987). 'Tales from Fernández Cubas: Adventure in the Fantastic', *Monographic Review/Revista monográfica* 3: 107–18.

Zatlin, Phyllis (1996). 'Amnesia, Strangulation, Hallucination and Other Mishaps: The Perils of Being Female in Tales of Cristina Fernández Cubas', *Hispania* 79: 36–44.

Zayas y Sotomayor, María de (1983). *Desengaños amorosos* (1647), ed. Alicia Yllera, Letras hispánicas 179 (Madrid: Cátedra).

Zipes, Jack (1984). *Breaking the Magic Spell: Radical Theories of Folk and Fairy-Tales* (New York: Methuen).

Zipes, Jack (1986). *Don't Bet on the Prince: Contemporary Feminist Fairy-Tales in North America and England* (New York: Methuen & Aldershot, Hants: Gower).

Zipes, Jack (1988). *Fairy-Tales and the Art of Subversion: The Classical Genre for Children and the Process of Civilization* (New York: Methuen; first edn 1983).

INDEX

Allende, Isabel (b. 1942, Chilean writer) 49

Almodóvar, Pedro (b. 1951, Spanish film-maker) 84

Alumbradismo 16

Álvarez, T. 16

Andersen, Hans Christian (Danish writer, 1805-75) 58-59, 63, 65, 67, 69-71

Apuleius, Lucius (123-ca 180, Latin poet and rhetorician) 32, 38-44

Arenal, E. 7

Aristophanes (ca 450-ca 385 BC, Athenian dramatist) 128

Aristotle (384-322 BC, philosopher) 128

Armas, F. A. de 44

Atencia, María Victoria (b. 1931, Spanish poet) x, 87, 90-91, 93, 97-98

Atwood, Margaret (b. 1939, Canadian poet, novelist, and critic) 116

Augustine, St (354-430, bp Hippo, Father of the Church) 23-24

Ayala-Dip, J.E. 82

Bachelard, Gaston (1884-1962, philosopher) x, 87-90, 92-98

Bakhtin, Mikhail Mikhailovich (1895-1975, Russian formalist philosopher) 22

Bandello, Matteo (1485-1561, Italian short-story writer) 44

Báñez, Domingo OP (1528-1604, confessor to Teresa of Avila) 17-19

Barbero Sánchez, Teresa (b. 1934, Spanish novelist) ix, 59-61

Barrie, James M. (1860-1937, Scots dramatist and writer) 59, 61-63, 66

Barthes, Roland (1915-80, French polymath) 21-23

Bartolomeo di Domenico OP (1343-?1415, ecclesiastical administrator and theologian) 25

Bataille, Georges (1897-1962, French philosopher) 113, 117

Baudrillard, J. 116

Beauvoir, Simone de (1908-86, French writer) 58

Bécquer, Gustavo Adolfo (1836-70, Spanish writer and poet) 87

Bellver, C. G. 73-76

Benet Goitia, Juan (1927-93, Spanish writer) 55-56

Bernabé de Palma 27-28

Bernhardt, Sarah (Henrietta Rosine Bernard, 1844-1923, French actress) 86

Bettelheim, B. 57

Birch, H. 127-28

Blanche of Bourbon (d. 1361, ma. Peter I of Castile 1353) 1

Bombal, María Luisa (1910-80, Chilean writer) 48-49

Botana, A. V. 80, 83-84

Bretz, M. L. 73

Brivic, S. 108

Brown, J. L. ix, 45-56

Bynum, C. W. 4, 6, 14

Cain, S. x

Cano, J. L. 52

Cano, Melchor (?1509-60, Dominican professor of theology and ecclesiastical politician) 17, 27, 29

Cardoso, L. 100

Carranza, Bartolomé de OP (1503-76, archbp Toledo) 27, 29

Carrera, E. vii-viii, 15-29

Carroll, Lewis (Charles Lutwidge Dodgson, 1832-98, writer and mathematician) 59-60

Carter, Angela (1940-95, British writer) 59, 116

Printed in Poland
by Amazon Fulfillment
Poland Sp. z o.o., Wrocław